the dailymash
Annual 2015

RANDOM ACTS OF FOUL-MOUTHED CRUELTY

Edited by: Neil Rafferty and Tim Telling

Written by
Daisy Buchanan, John Camm, John Foster, Suzy Houston, Jennifer McKenzie,
Nick Pettigrew, Neil Rafferty, David Stubbs, Tim Telling, Tom Whiteley, Paul Watson

Mash Books

Launched in April 2007, the Daily Mash is Britain's
biggest satire website providing a daily diet of spoof
stories, commentary and opinion on national and
international news and sport.

www.thedailymash.co.uk

An Hachette UK Company
www.hachette.co.uk

First published in Great Britain in 2014 by
Hamlyn, a division of Octopus Publishing Group Ltd
Endeavour House
189 Shaftesbury Avenue
London
WC2H 8JY
www.octopusbooks.co.uk

Produced by Mash Books, an imprint of Mashed Productions Ltd and The Daily Mash.
www.thedailymash.co.uk

ISBN 978-0-600-62975-7

A CIP catalogue record for this book is available from the British Library

Printed and bound in Spain

1 3 5 7 9 10 8 6 4 2

Design and picture research:

MiCHaEL GiLL DesigN LtD.

www.michaelgill.eu

Picture credits
Front cover:
    John Stillwell/PA Archive/Press Association Images
    REX/Richard Austin
  5 Andrew Matthews/PA Wire
 15 Sean Dempsey/PA Wire
 18 Stefan Rousseau/PA Wire/Press Association Images
 18 DPA/DPA/Press Association Images
 22 Universal/courtesy Everett Collection
 24 REX/Colin Davey
 26 Stefan Rousseau/PA Wire
 26 AP Photo/Lefteris Pitarakis
 27 Kirsty Wigglesworth/AP/Press Association Images
 30 Sang Tan/AP/Press Association Images
 34 REX/Frank Micelotta
 37 Jeff Moore/Jeff Moore/Empics Entertainment
 41 Andrew Matthews/PA Archive/Press Association Images
 48 Rex/ITV
 44 David Iliff/Wikimedia Commons

 44 The Illustrated London News
 44 AG Gymnasium Melle/Wikimedia Commons
 44 Elgaard/Wikimedia Commons
 48 Doug Peters/EMPICS Entertainment
 49 Yui Mok/PA Wire
 56 Tim Ireland/PA Archive/Press Association Images
 59 The Illustrated London News
 69 Yui Mok/PA Archive/Press Association Images
 81 Paolo Aguilar/EFE/Press Association Images
 91 Szwarc Henri/ABACA/Press Association Images
 96 DEAN LEWINS/AAP/Press Association Images
101 David Davies/PA Wire
108 REX/James McCauley
109 Andrew Milligan/PA Wire

All other pictures:
Dreamstime, iStock, PhotoDisc,
The Illustrated London News and designers' own.

the dailymash

www.thedailymash.co.uk   **RANDOM ACTS OF FOUL-MOUTHED CRUELTY**   Monday 2014

MARRIED GAYS TO TOUR DROUGHT-HIT COUNTRIES

Betrothed homosexuals are to use their magical flood-creating powers to bring new life to desert regions

GAY people in civil partnerships, who have been granted the power to summon rainstorms from the heavens by God and UKIP, plan to use it benevolently.

Nathan Muir, who saw storm clouds forming as he kissed his husband on their wedding day, said: "We're honeymooning in Sub-Saharan Africa so that we can bring the waters of gayness to its parched landscape.

"If one small kiss summons a full-on pea souper imagine what fully penetrative gay intercourse could do."

He added: "A lot of people think God dislikes homosexuals, but if that's so why did he give us supernatural powers?

"Apparently he destroyed Sodom by sending loads of fire and brimstone, but those things are very useful in the right amounts.

"If Sodom's level of gay sex had been just a fraction lower it would've been kept snugly warm. The moral is that God's fine with moderate amounts of gay sex."

Homosexuals are being welcomed in drought-prone regions, with Australia's Irri-GAY-Tion chain of honeymoon hotels in the Outback paying couples $2,500 a night. And in Africa, gay marriages are the new craze among farmers keen to provide for their families.

Ethiopian Abdu said: "They say homosexuality is an abomination in God's sight, but on the other hand walking seven miles a day for drinking water sucks pretty hard too."

Healthy breakfast eater's life still shit

Office worker Tom Logan's life is still shit despite him eating a nutritious breakfast every day.

LOGAN claims his commitment to eating a breakfast packed with fresh fruit and nourishing whole grains has done nothing to improve his miserable existence.

He said: "People always stress the importance of a healthy breakfast as if eating a few bits of fruit is some magical elixir of happiness.

"But I still work in commission-only telesales, spend every night sitting on my own in the pub reading spy books, and haven't kissed a woman on the lips since 2007.

"I've got the same tedious routine, except I'm living it with a few more vitamins in my bloodstream. Certainly I'm no-one's definition of a 'winner'.

"Apparently all those hours I spent poaching eggs and forcing down bitter, slimy grapefruit were a complete fucking waste of time.

"I may as well have had a Mars bar and a fag, washed down with a can of lager."

Professor Henry Brubaker, of the Institute for Studies, said: "Breakfast's ability to positively influence everything is wildly overrated. It's just several handfuls of food you'd never consider eating at a more civilised time of day.

"The habit of eating porridge only came into existence because a tired woman mistook some oats for a cup of tea and poured milk onto them.

"The results were disgusting but she just shrugged and poured them down her throat because who gives a shit when you're late for work."

A vitamin-packed prelude to tedium

Miliband: "I had sex with a woman"

LABOUR leader Ed Miliband has claimed to have done it with a girl.

The unsolicited admission followed allegations of sexual behaviour by left-wing alpha males Tony Blair and Bill Clinton.

Miliband said: "I'm too much of a gentleman to reveal her name, but I will tell you that she was ideologically committed to solving issues of unequal wealth distribution.

"We met when I was 24 and attending a summer camp for social democratic teenagers in Sweden. I could pass for 18 at the time, I was a late developer.

"Inflamed by late-night discussion of a pan-European carbon emissions trading scheme, we took ourselves into the woods and made love. It was like an erotic scene in a film.

"Afterwards I couldn't find one of my socks."

Prince George rejects Christianity

THE heir to the throne thinks Christianity is a load of nonsense, it has emerged.

The infant was left bitter and angry after being dressed up like a tiny old lady and baptised against his wishes.

Desperately flailing his plump limbs, the future king said: "Get … off … me … I have no interest in your strange, outmoded belief system!"

He continued: "If it was up to me, I'd probably choose to worship the Egyptian gods, particularly Horus.

"He's a super-muscly guy with a bird's head. That's the sort of tangible superhero god a young boy can relate to.

"I can also see myself getting into tarots, crystals and occultism. Perhaps I will be the next Aleister Crowley."

Tired of being invisible

Dreadlocked caucasians demand to face more discrimination

White people with dreadlocks are not facing as much discrimination as they would ideally like, it has emerged.

MATTED hair owners claim that other than being broadly defined as 'crusties' and 'trustafarians' they were going largely unnoticed by mainstream society.

25-year-old Brighton resident Tom Logan, who prefers to be called Boz, said: "I can't remember the last time someone shouted something in the street, and even then it was something non-committal like 'have a bath mate'.

"Can't they see that I don't subscribe to their stupid materialist values, and am in fact a threat to the status quo?

"These dreads took years to grow, they're bloody itchy, and right now I'm feeling like it was all a waste of time."

Dreadlocked Emma Bradford, aka Trouser, said: "I've been able to get a series of jobs, nothing fancy admittedly and mostly in organic cafés but still I'm consistently being treated like a normal, unremarkable person ... which I'm not, obviously, because I've got unusual hair and a rusty van with pictures of animals on it. Also I can stay upright on a unicycle for up to three minutes at a time."

She added: "Clearly someone needs to oppress me. Maybe they could bring back punks just so they can chase us around town centres."

"Perhaps your concern could extend to not eating us", say chickens

CHICKENS have thanked consumers for their concern over methods of slaughter and asked if that goodwill could be extended to just leaving them alone.

As Pizza Express confirmed all their chicken meat is halal, Britain's favourite birds stressed that being stunned before having their throats cut in the traditional Muslim fashion was 'small consolation', and that, ideally, they would prefer to live in an orchard.

Jane Thomson, a four-month-old chicken from Lincolnshire, said: "If I was a Pizza Express customer I'd probably want to know if they were using religious methods of slaughter, but it's a moot point because I'm not a huge fan of pizza and I'm a prisoner in this massive shed.

"Still, it's nice to know that before you shove me and all of my friends into your fat faces, you're terribly worried about how we spend our last moments. You're an amazing species and our admiration for you is boundless."

Ms Thomson added: "Funnily enough, the humans who spend their meagre salaries at the popular chicken outlets are the ones with whom we feel the greatest affinity.

"Perhaps one day we'll all live together in a big orchard and you can give us corn and we'll give you eggs and no-one needs to die.

"Anyway, that's my tuppence worth."

We fly in a 'V' because it looks brilliant, say birds

Birds have revealed they fly in a V-formation because it looks 'classy'.

SCIENTISTS claimed the shape was caused by maximising 'lift' from the bird in front, but birds said they just like to pretend they are in the Red Arrows.

Martin Bishop, a goose, said: "We could fly in a circle if we wanted to. Circles are a doddle, but it would look weird. Like a massive, floating hole.

"The V-shape is what we geese call a 'design classic'. It's simple and beautiful but it's also a dynamic statement of intent. It screams 'progress!'."

Bishop added: "When you're flying in 'the V' you feel like a goddamn master of the universe. I've done it maybe a hundred times

and every time I do it I look over at my mate Brian and shout 'this is totally brilliant, we're so cool'."

Bishop's friend, Brian Stevens, said: "What I don't understand is why humans shoot at us. Would you shoot at the Red Arrows?

"No, you fucking wouldn't."

Stolen Damien Hirst artworks 'easily replaced'

A WEST London painter and decorator has offered to replace the two Damien Hirst artworks stolen from an art gallery.

Norman Steele says he is the ideal person to create new versions of the two works because he keeps all his sample pots in his van.

He continued: "Circles of household paint in a regular pattern on a blank white canvas? I can get those done for you by lunchtime, and for less than £33,000.

"A lot less, if we're talking cash in hand."

Middle-aged man 'was wearing non-Superdry clothing'

"It was like a work shirt or something"

A 42-YEAR-OLD male was chased by other middle-aged men after attending a barbecue wearing a shirt that was not from Superdry.

Father-of-one Tom Logan opted to wear a plain button-down shirt instead of a garment bearing the Superdry logo with Japanese characters spelling out the words 'increasing girth'.

Logan said: "Just because I'm slightly past my prime doesn't mean I have to wear quasi-youthful clothes with writing on, even if everyone else does.

"I underestimated the fury it would provoke."

Logan's work colleague Roy Hobbs said: "At first I was ok with it, although his shirt seemed kind of strange and old-fashioned.

"But as the afternoon wore on I became increasingly angry. Does he not like Superdry or something? Does he think he's too good for Britain's top casualwear brand?"

"Maybe I'd have been ok with it if he'd worn a shirt or jumper from Fat Face, White Stuff or O'Neill. But he had to go the attention-seeking 'plain shirt' route."

Onlookers described the mood towards Logan growing increasingly hostile, until a burger was thrown at his back.

Hobbs said: "That was the trigger for the primal rage. The other, normal, Superdry dads started hooting and lobbing things, first sausages and baps but then large stones.

"We chased him onto the roof of the garage with a vague idea of dragging him down then burning him on the barbecue.

"But then our wives got angry and we had to stop."

What about Keith fucking Richards? Nigella asks America

NIGELLA Lawson has asked the US how come she gets barred but Keith Richards wanders in and out like he owns the place.

The TV chef was stopped from boarding a flight to Los Angeles because she admitted to taking cocaine, prompting her to ask customs officials 'if they were out of their fucking minds'.

She added: "Keith Richards would have regarded the amount of cocaine I took as invisible. It would not have registered on his consciousness. He's probably still got that much stuck up there and he just can't be bothered to have it removed.

"And yet he has a house in America. I implore you, look at him and look at me and then explain to me what the fuck you are talking about."

Half-arsed Trophies & Medals

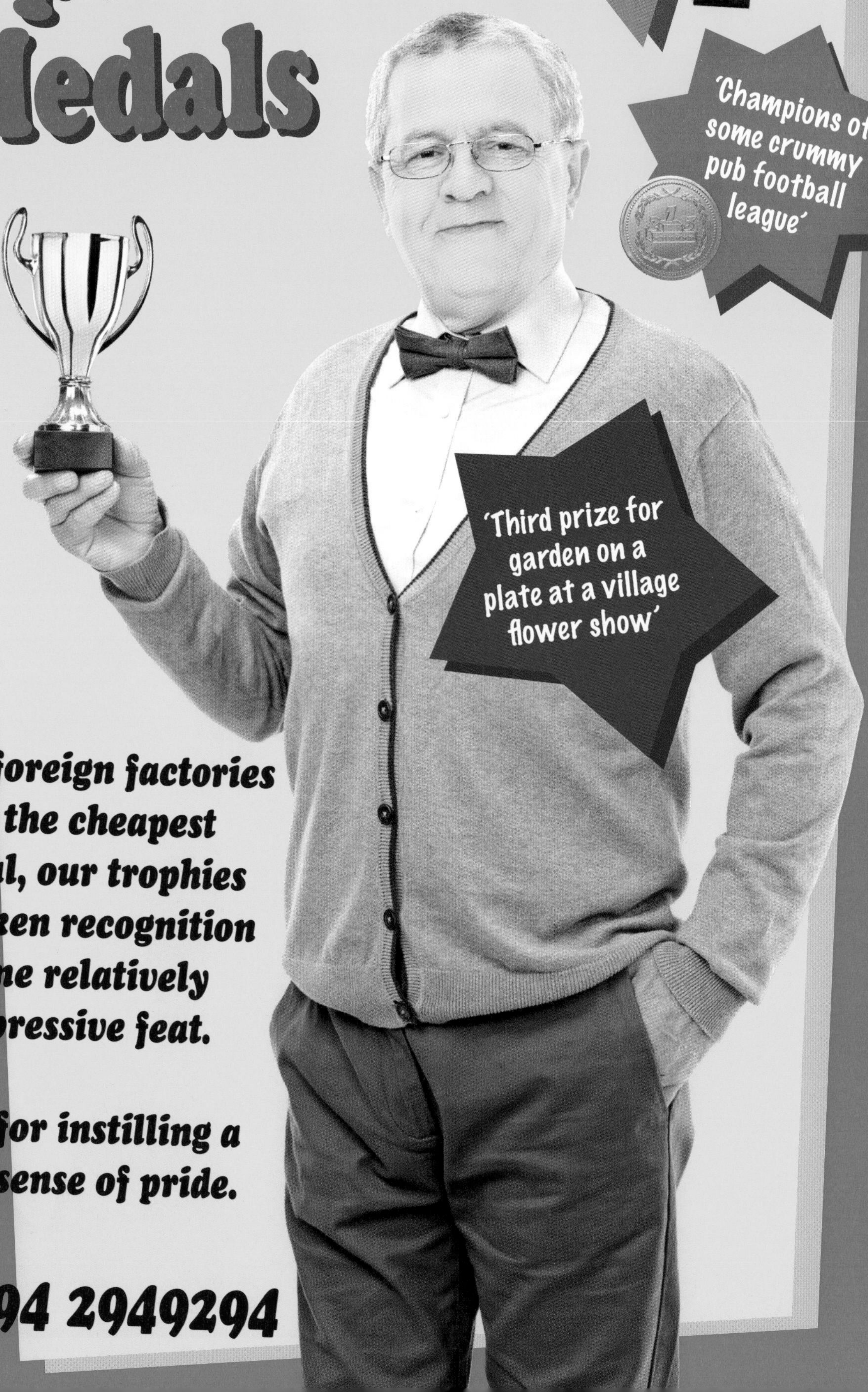

'Skittles winners by default because the other team didn't turn up'

'Champions of some crummy pub football league'

'Third prize for garden on a plate at a village flower show'

Made in foreign factories using the cheapest material, our trophies are a token recognition of some relatively unimpressive feat.

Perfect for instilling a limited sense of pride.

Tel: 0594 2949294

Facebook launches Schadenfreude button

Facebook has launched a feature allowing people to express pleasure when friends post bad news.

MANY users had been anxious about being misconstrued as sympathetic for liking posts about illness, house buying problems or pet death.

A spokesman said: "The success of our social network is built on the satisfaction users get from seeing old enemies and rivals fail. I'm actually amazed it has taken us this long to fully exploit that fact."

She added: "When a poster gets over 10 Schadenfreude clicks, we can send an automated message to their listed spouse or partner highlighting how unpopular they are.

"We then offer them a break-up pack where we change their relationship status for them and send their now ex-partner a sad bear emoji."

Facebook user Tom Logan said: "My mate is just about to get divorced – well, I say mate, he fingered my girlfriend when we were 17 and they ended up getting married – so this couldn't have come at a better time."

"I hope it hurt"

Guardian begins annual ruining of Christmas

THE *Guardian* newspaper has launched its annual appeal to make you feel dreadful about Christmas.

Unveiling a miserable George Monbiot article about how having nice things is bad, editor Alan Rusbridger pledged to 'gnaw at our readers' consciences like they will gnaw at the bones of horribly abused poultry'.

The paper is lining up a series of nasty, depressing yuletide features including excerpts from Jonathan Freedland's new book *It is Not a*

Wonderful Life, Polly Toynbee's *Guide to Turning a Nice Christmas Dinner into an Argument About Universal Benefits* and a Nick Cohen article about reactionary toys made by lovely, tiny dogs.

Rusbridger said: "The only good thing capitalism has ever done is to turn Christmas into a secular indulgence instead of a credulous rehashing of manipulative, Iron Age fairy stories.

"We're going to put that on a tea towel that you can give to your gran."

It has children, you know

ALL PEOPLE THROWN OUT OF NIGHTCLUBS WERE TREATED UNFAIRLY

Everyone who has ever been thrown out of a nightclub has confirmed it was not their fault.

THE Institute for Studies found that everyone forcibly removed from a late-night venue was not doing anything, and the bouncers were just being pricks.

Professor Henry Brubaker said: "The problem lies with club management, who are always looking for an excuse to throw paying customers out on the street.

"Britons don't want any trouble and weren't starting anything, it was just a misunderstanding. Even if it looked bad at the time, they should have been given a chance to explain."

Emma Bradford, 29, was thrown out of a London bar last year: "I was upset because my fish died so I went in the cubicle with three friends so they could comfort me.

"We all felt very sad which is why we came out sniffing."

Tom Logan, 24, was thrown out of Velvet nightclub in Kent after allegedly exposing himself on the dance floor.

He said: "My penis was briefly visible, but I only took off my trousers because they were chafing, which is the venue's fault for having a 'no jeans' dress code.

"At least I think they do. If not it was just that Welsh bouncer who hates me for no reason, being a bastard."

Professor Brubaker agreed: "Tom's friends and relatives all agree that he's a 'good kiddie' and 'sound' so he definitely couldn't be in the wrong."

Not what it looks like

Kate Bush warns everyone she now looks like Lemmy

KATE Bush has announced her first live shows for 35 years but warned fans she is not quite the same.

The reclusive *Wuthering Heights* star said that while she had continued to 'explore' her creative landscape' she had forgotten to moisturise since 1987.

She added: "I'm an obsessive artist so I can spend months hunched over a piano in the dark, stopping only to wolf down a Monster Munch sandwich and a two-litre bottle of Tizer.

"The point is, I look like Lemmy now. It took a bit of getting used to, but now I prefer it.

"Anyway, I've written 52 songs about butterflies which I think you're going to enjoy."

FEATURE

The Daily Mash Guide to ...
Snake vs Crocodile

A blow-by-blow account of the reptile battle that has captivated the internet

1

2

The struggle between an anaconda and a crocodile in a Queensland Lake has captured the public's imagination in a way no story about war or famine ever could.

Experts from the Institute for Studies were on hand to document the brutal majesty of two things that are quite like dinosaurs having a fight.

1. The approach

The snake is basking in the lake, minding its own business. It seems at peace, like a martial arts master. But here comes a bunch of young male crocodiles, drunk and looking for trouble and teasing the snake for not having any legs. The snake ignores them but they just won't leave it, these crocodiles have got something to prove.

2. The grapple

The cockiest crocodile oversteps the line by biting a chunk out of the snake's arse, or more technically its rear end. The snake immediately coils around it like a massive Slinky spring. The croc's jaws are pinned shut so it balls its stumpy claws into fists and starts punching the snake, which has no effect. Then it starts kicking the snake in the side with its little legs – also ineffective. At this point the crocodile is pretty much fucked.

3. The swallow

The snake dislocates its massive jaws and swallows the crocodile whole in a disgusting act of gluttony that makes onlooking birds retch. However the size of the crocodile is such that the snake's skin is stretched absurdly tightly and it looks like a crocodile covered in snakeskin. So the snake does now kind of have legs, an irony which is probably lost on the crocodile as it is slowly but inexorably digested.

3

Your problems solved, with *Holly Harper*

Should I get a swastika tattooed on my face?

Dear Holly,
I'm supposed to be the biggest badass in One Direction, but now everyone thinks Louis and Zayn are the bollocks just because they smoked what the newspapers are calling 'a roll-up blunt cigarette joint'. I was thinking of having a swastika tattooed on my face just to remind everyone that I am far more hardcore than those other four middle-class pansies. What do you think?
Harry Styles
1D Tour Bus

Dear Harry,
When I grow up I'm going to be a rebel. I'll do bad stuff like give the finger to lollipop ladies and do massive burps at the dinner table and leave supermarket trolleys in the wrong place. My dad does all these things and he's really naughty. He even once called my granny a 'satanic bitch' behind her back. She didn't hear him though so I helped him out by shouting it for him really loud so that everyone in the post office could hear.
Hope that helps!
Holly xx

I am torn between these two lovely cars

Dear Holly,
I'm finding it hard to choose between the Toyota GT86 and the Subaru BRZ because they're both so similar and there's not much difference in price. How should I go about helping viewers of *Top Gear* decide between these two vehicles?
Jeremy Clarkson
Chipping Norton

Dear Jeremy,
At my school we tend to make all critical decisions via children's folklore and counting rhymes. We also ward off contagious diseases, bad luck and death with cross-keys and use hopscotch to predict the future. Sadly I am not sure there is a skipping rhyme potent enough to cure an ageing, bitter man of his deep-seated personality problems or his fashion sense.
Hope that helps!
Holly xx

Your astrological week ahead, with Psychic Bob

Aries
21 MAR-19 APR
You should take time each day to gather your thoughts. Eight seconds should be plenty.

Taurus
20 APR – 20 MAY
Your upbeat outlook, ready smile and eternal optimism are just three reasons why everyone loathes you.

Gemini
21 MAY-20 JUN
So it turns out your old schoolfriend Adam actually didn't win the Mercury Music Prize in 1998. The lying little bastard.

Cancer
21 JUN-22 JUL
Life is a cabaret, old chum. Expensive, disappointing and much better in the 1920s.

Leo
23 JUL-22 AUG
You love your cat, she's just like a little human being that tortures small animals and likes the taste of their own rectum.

Virgo
23 AUG-22 SEP
You reek of Taurus. Into the bath with you. Chop-chop.

Libra
23 SEP-23 OCT
Watching Adrian Chiles on the television this week, you're faced with the awful mental image of what he must look like bending over to dry his feet after a shower.

Scorpio
24 OCT-21 NOV
Flying over a desert island this week, you see that somebody has spelled out the name of their favourite Beatles album in pebbles on the beach. Good for them.

Sagittarius
22 NOV-21 DEC
If you need to be told not to vote on a repeat of a reality TV show, maybe it's a good idea you don't vote for anything.

Capricorn
22 DEC-19 JAN
A bad day at the park on Saturday as you try recreating the Diet Coke ad, but the can explodes in the lawnmower blades giving the hunky gardener aluminium shrapnel in his face.

Aquarius
20 JAN-19 FEB
You're the one with the bucket, right?

Pisces
20 FEB-20 MAR
When describing World War One as 'lions led by donkeys', people tend to forget how awesome that would actually look.

Enjoy Outside

Bored of the internet and telly?
Want to try something different?
Why not go outside*

Outside is the larger alternative to your living room. There's sky instead of roof, grass instead of carpet and sun instead of radiators.

Other features of outside:
Trees • Foxes • Strangers • Builders • The sea • Trains • Bridges • Mice

To learn more about outside, visit
www.gooutside.com

*WARNING: Outside may cause panic

DJ talks about his work as if it has artistic merit

Like a musical instrument that's not a musical instrument

A dance music DJ has spoken about his work like he's some sort of artist.

28-YEAR-OLD Stephen Malley earns good money playing CDs of house music to people on drugs.

Making a thoughtful facial expression, he said: "With me, it's more of a journey.

"I could start techy and then go more progressive, or start progressive and then go trancey.

"I'm like this crazy chameleon figure, always changing, always unpredictable."

Seemingly oblivious to his role as a temporary figurehead for the most easily entertained demographic on earth, he continued: "Lots of DJs do this thing where they take the bass out for a little bit then drop it back in.

"But I take the bass out for quite a long time, then bring it back in.

"It's the future."

Malley confirmed that he was also working on his first album, or at least getting some other people to make it for him so that he could put his name on it.

He added: "When I've achieved all my goals as a DJ, I'll probably write a book that redefines literature, or do a science course and then build the first actual teleporter.

"But who knows? Like I said, I'm a chameleon."

Stop calling it your money, says RBS

THE Royal Bank of Scotland has reminded customers that 'their' money is actually its money.

The bank said giving people access to their accounts is not a core priority.

An RBS spokesman explained: "Stop whining that you can't get money out.

"We need that cash for gambling on the international markets, profiting from

commodity speculation and paying our brokers' bonuses.

"You need it for buying celebrity autobiographies and bath salts. I think we can both agree which is more important."

Being cool and being a parent not compatible

He thinks they're 'friends' but they aren't

It is not possible to be cool and a parent, experts have warned.

AN increase in magazines and websites for stylish 'upscale' child owners has fuelled a delusion that people with kids are something other than exhausted sewage workers.

Sociologist Mary Fisher said: "In previous generations we accepted that once you had kids you were basically dead.

"Fashion, music and art were no longer for you because you were so tired and had spent all your money on plastic animals.

"In a way that's part of the reason for being a parent, that you no longer only care about your stupid self and idiotic consumer bullshit."

The Institute for Studies confirmed that it is not possible to be cool and a parent.

Professor Henry Brubaker said:

"Young people decide who's cool. And did you ever look at your dad, asleep in a chair, and think 'wow you're so cool'.

"Even if you're a parent with a big house full of antlers and art books, and you've got £400 jeans, you're not cool.

"You're old and weird, you probably like Gwyneth Paltrow and are certainly an idiot."

Bright poor kids work out they're probably fucked

MANY poorer pupils are bright enough to understand their own limited prospects, it has emerged.

A new study of social mobility found bright, poor children understood their place in the social hierarchy just as well as their public school counterparts.

Tom Booker, an 11-year-old state school pupil, said: "I've done some research in my spare time, and basically everyone in a position of power seems to have gone to a fee-paying school.

"And our politicians don't seem clever, in fact they're dicks, so I guess it is who you know.

"If I bust my arse I might get to be an assistant bank manager, which doesn't really appeal, so I'll probably get into drugs."

Put cancer in e-cigarettes, say non-smokers

Non-smokers would prefer electronic cigarettes to be fatal, it has been confirmed.

SMOKING abstainers are calling for e-cigarettes to contain deadly and debilitating chemicals to allow them to continue to feel smug.

Non-smoker Tom Logan said: "My neighbour has a much better job than me and a far more attractive girlfriend, but as he's a smoker I could always take comfort in the thought of him dying an agonising death.

"Recently however he started using e-cigarettes, so now he probably won't have a leg amputated or get lung cancer.

"His clothes don't stink, I never see him shivering out in the garden and if anything he's smoking more.

"I definitely think they should put cancer in e-cigarettes. That or something worse, like bubonic plague or toxic waste that makes you turn into a monster."

Office manager Donna Sheridan agreed: "I've had to start hanging around crack houses to feel better than others.

"But I keep getting my purse stolen and if you're not interested in crack they really don't have much else to talk about."

She won't even get ash on her fancy fancy clothes

Daily Mail hates everyone in Britain

THE *Daily Mail* hates Britain and everyone in it, experts have confirmed.

The Institute for Studies was unable to identify a single demographic that the Mail does not loathe with a pathological intensity and concluded that the paper was engaged in a form of 'psychological terrorism'.

Professor Henry Brubaker said: "Obviously, you start with immigrants and those descended from immigrants. But then you have young people, poor people, rich people – particularly the famous ones – and, of course, women.

"If you read the *Mail* for about nine seconds you can see the extent to which they despise women utterly.

"If you're a working mother you're a selfish whore, but if you stay at home you're going to become severely depressed and morbidly obese.

"And if you're even vaguely ambivalent about abortion, they would prefer it if you just drank some Mr Muscle."

Professor Brubaker added: "And don't make the mistake of thinking they're fond of old people. They take great delight in scaring the absolute shit out of them.

"Even the Royal Family is loathed. They grasp any opportunity to publish photos of Princess Beatrice looking like a very special kind of moron.

"Meanwhile, they're clearly looking forward to dismembering Kate Middleton over the next five to 10 years."

Mohammed Iqbal, a fundamentalist Muslim cleric from Deptford, said: "I hate Britain and everything it stands for.

"But even I look at the *Daily Mail* and think 'that's just nasty'."

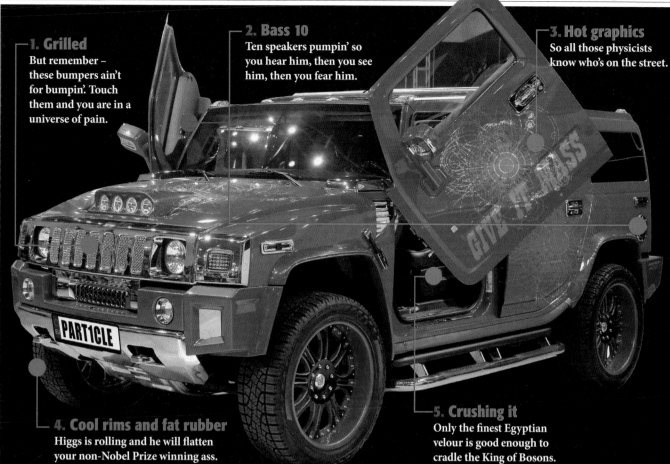

1. Grilled
But remember – these bumpers ain't for bumpin'. Touch them and you are in a universe of pain.

2. Bass 10
Ten speakers pumpin' so you hear him, then you see him, then you fear him.

3. Hot graphics
So all those physicists know who's on the street.

4. Cool rims and fat rubber
Higgs is rolling and he will flatten your non-Nobel Prize winning ass.

5. Crushing it
Only the finest Egyptian velour is good enough to cradle the King of Bosons.

PROF HIGGS SPENDS NOBEL PRIZE MONEY ON PIMPED-OUT SUV

Nobel laureate Peter Higgs has spent his prize money on a customised lilac sports utility vehicle.

The emeritus professor of theoretical physics at Edinburgh University said: "I've dropped some serious Nobel cheddar on this bad boy.

"It's sick."

Higgs, who is currently deliberating between the license plates PART1CLE or H1GG5, said: "In the place where I grew up, physics was the only route out.

"I saw neighbourhood physicists in their sports cars and designer clothes and thought yeah, I gotta get some theories.

"My new ride is representing. I'm going to fill it with the best goddamn cognac and some sweet, sweet honies.

"And then I'm going to park it outside Hawking's house and play my Nobel acceptance speech louder than a motherfucker."

PARENTS WARNED TO STOP CALLING THEIR CHILDREN LILY OR JACK

British parents' desire to give all children the name Jack or Lily could have sociological repercussions, experts have warned.

RESEARCHERS believe that over-reliance on the two reassuringly middle-class names could cause practical and psychological problems.

Sociologist Donna Sheridan said: "The names Jack and Lily have gone beyond the point of popularity to become a national epidemic.

"We're starting to see primary schools where 98% of pupils are called Jack or Lily, resulting in teachers being unable to address any of their pupils individually.

"In one Year 3 class, all the boys completely ostracised the only one not called Jack, a boy called Ian. Or as they called him, 'the un-Jack'.

"I believe they have been making plans to drown him."

Teacher Mary Fisher said: "My class consists of Lilys numbers 1-12 and Jacks 1-14, for example I might say 'Jack 3 give Jack 9 his pencil back.'"

Sheridan warned that if the trend continues it will become impossible for anyone to ever be completely sure who was speaking to them.

Parent Stephen Malley said: "I have to admit it can be quite confusing having three sons

Tiny helpless clones

called Jack and two daughters called Lily, but it's infinitely preferable to not calling them Jack or Lily.

"I can't imagine what it would be like having a child called Richard or Emma. We'd have

to put them up for adoption, although I doubt anyone would want them with those names.

"If we have another child we'll probably have to give them a different name though. Maybe Lily-Jack."

Stupid poor people are stupid and poor, says massive blonde-haired child

THE debate over social mobility was reignited last night thanks to an opinion from an economy-sized boy.

Boris Johnson, London's six-year-old mayor, said that stupid poor people are all stupid and poor, apart from the few that are surprisingly clever.

Boris said: "The poor clever ones should be allowed to be clever. But I've counted and there are only sev-

en of them, so all the clever schools will have enough room.

"The stupid ones will always be stupid and they should go to a thick school with dense teachers and write down all the wrong answers with idiot pencils.

"Then, when they grow up, they can do all the stupid jobs while the clever people do all the clever jobs."

Delivering the Margaret Thatcher Lecture at the Centre for Policy Studies, he added: "So, what I am saying is, all the rich people are clever and all the poor people are stupid.

"Apart from the seven poor people who are not stupid.

"My job is a clever job. I get to wear a lot of different helmets."

"Stupid people jobs are easier than clever people jobs"

They may as well be playing tennis on a dual carriageway

Roads not a velodrome

Britain's roads are not a specialist cycle racing facility, it has been confirmed.

IMPROVED weather has prompted large groups of emotionless drones with huge waxed legs to stage weekend cycle competitions on the country's highways.

However, officials have confirmed that roads are really designed for travel rather than amateur sporting events involving large clusters of wobbly people.

A government spokesman said: "Since Roman times, roads have been principally for the transportation of people and goods from point A to point B, rather than for buggering about on.

"Cycling is fine if you're going on a legitimate journey, but if you're just pointlessly 'testing yourself' against a group of similarly bored accountants it would be really good to keep that to a designated facility.

"You know those oval-shaped tracks you see on the Olympics, the ones that are designed for, and used exclusively for, bike racing?

"Well, you can book one for an hourly rate, it's quite affordable if everyone in a group chips in."

Car driver Emma Bradford said: "Horse riders can be a bit frustrating but at least they don't do it on the A46.

"I find amateur cycle race people rather hard to like, except the fat one who's miles behind all the others. I feel sorry for him and admire his tenacity."

You can have the fucking place, Britain tells Romania

BRITAIN has offered to swap countries with Romania.

The sodden northern European hellhole has said that all the Romanians can come and live here if we can go and live there.

A Downing Street spokesman said David Cameron has written to the government in Bucharest, saying: "You want it? Have it. Have

Brighton, England

every shitty fucking square inch of it.

"It's yours. Enjoy."

The spokesman added: "I'm rather looking forward to being

Mamaia, Romania

Romanian. The Black Sea has some beautiful resorts, but you can also go up into the mountains and pretend to be Dracula."

BBC's Musketeers adaptation is slammed for lack of dog characters

NEW BBC series *The Musketeers* has been condemned for portraying Alexandre Dumas's characters as human rather than canine.

Viewer Roy Hobbs said: "When I heard the BBC was doing a big-budget live-action adaptation of this classic tale of hound courage, I was like 'wow, real dogs in leatherwear having sword fights'.

"But they're just people, even the character of Milady de Winter is portrayed by an actual lady rather than a sexy cat."

FEATURE

Michael Gove's ...
history lesson

Good morning class. I'm Michael Gove: much loved former education secretary, next prime minister and the man who puts the Gove in government.

Some people – lefties, historians, a 25-year-old sitcom I've only just heard of – have been getting history wrong. Here's what actually happened.

1. World War One:

The lie that our troops were "lions led by donkeys" must be overturned. In truth, the lions were the visionary members of the officer class who invented the revolutionary tactic of swamping the enemy's machine guns with donkey bodies.

2. Wilfred Owen

The poet's famous line "Gas! Quick boys, an ecstasy of fumbling," wasn't inspired by a mustard gas attack but by a fellow soldier good-naturedly breaking wind in his face as a joke, the whinger.

3. The Crusades

Basically a Christian outreach programme, like the Salvation Army, which delivered improving leaflets to the benighted heathens of the Middle East. Created the wonderful reputation white people still enjoy in the region today.

4. The Revolutionary War

Historians claim that Britain and America fought each other in this war, but that could never have happened because we're both the goodies. Clearly some kind of administrative mistake.

5. World War Two

Evidence that the Soviet Union defeated the Nazis on the Eastern Front is obviously false, because they were Communists and only a nation built on free-market principles with privatised utilities could be successful.

6. Dunkirk

Revisionists have called this a British retreat, but actually it was more like an early D-Day but a little bit slower and slightly more backwards.

7. Italia '90

BBC lies that Chris Waddle kicked a crucial penalty into the sky have been disproved by amateur historians on the *Daily Telegraph*'s comment desk, who uncovered new evidence that he buried it in the net and England beat Argentina in the final.

VENGEANCE FOR PONIES

Every year thousands of ponies die unnecessarily. In too many cases these deaths go unavenged.

Your money will hire implacable professional assassins with state-of-the-art firearms.

Already this year we have avenged 685 pony deaths

Brian Wade
48
Cruel
Farmer

Marcus Price
21
Didn't feed
his pony

Mary Fisher
28
Too fat to ride her
pony but did it
anyway

SHOT

BLOWN UP

PUSHED OFF A CLIFF

IT'S WHAT THE PONIES WOULD HAVE WANTED

Paypal donations to vengeanceforponies@hotmail.com

Women impressed by men who condemn their taste in music

Women have confirmed that nothing gets them hotter than men vigorously criticising the music they listen to.

RESEARCHERS at the Institute for Studies found that women experience strong sexual impulses towards men who glance through their iTunes playlist while mouthing the words 'shit, shit, shit'.

When condemnation of their favourite artists is then followed up with recommendations of obscure beard rock albums, most women are unable to stop themselves initiating sexual intercourse.

Highly attractive woman Carolyn Ryan said: "When a guy asks me what's on my iPod then tells me that I've been fooled into thinking I like Emeli Sandé by marketing, then he has my full attention, upstairs and downstairs.

"If he then proceeds to rank Radiohead albums from worst to best then it's pretty much on, and we're doing it while he's explain-

ing that *Amnesiac* is perennially underrated."

Model Helen Archer agreed: "When I see men who nod their head attentively to the music but never, ever get on the dancefloor because music's far too serious a passion for them, I immediately crave their genetic material."

94% of women surveyed admitted that they couldn't respect a man who didn't launch into a rant about musical authenticity whenever he heard The Saturdays.

Dissenting voice Joanna Kramer said: "Obviously I know Katy Perry is shit. But it is much, much better for having a dance to on a Friday night than the collected catalogue of Rush."

Hoping to attract a dominant prog rock fan

America spied on Yorkshire 'for about five minutes'

AMERICA'S National Security Agency tapped the phone calls of Yorkshire for five minutes before throwing its headphones across the room in horror.

Seasoned professionals at the NSA, many of whom have spied on the French, were left traumatised by their brief insight into what Yorkshire people say to each other in private.

A source said: "It was like overhearing a conversation between demons from the fifth circle of hell.

"No matter where the conversation started out, it very quickly found its way to the subject of faeces.

"They were talking about it as if it was money."

Britney Spears espouses Karl Marx's theory of labour as value

BRITNEY Spears has admitted her latest single *Work Bitch* is inspired by the writings of Karl Marx.

The star has based her latest hit on a lifetime's study of the father of communism, and a strong desire to champion the cause of the proletariat.

She said: "I've always sung about the relationship between people and the economic systems which

govern their lives, for example my exploration of the seductive power of capital in *Gimme More*.

"*Work Bitch* is a satire of commodity fetishism which underlines that the real owners of the means of production are the workers themselves.

"When I whip a woman wearing bondage gear in the video, it's a metaphor."

FEATURE

Phil Neville's guide to ...
Rio

1. Copacabana Beach

The sand is very white, being made up of small particles of white rock and seems to stretch for miles, which is because it does stretch for miles. The average temperature can be as high as 31 degrees or as low as 19 degrees and sometimes it can be 23 degrees. Or 28.

2. Christ The Redeemer Statue

The statue is 98 foot tall, which is the same as 16 people who are six foot tall. Plus another two feet. It was built between 1922 and 1931, which is nine years, not quite as long as I played for Manchester United. Manchester United is a club in the North of England, which has no statues of Christ taller than 80 feet. I don't think so, anyway.

3. Currency

The national currency of Brazil is the real, as in 'Real Madrid' or 'Real Gone Kid', which is my favourite song to sing at karaoke. Karaoke is Japanese rather than Brazilian, but I'm sure they probably have karaoke bars over here. I've been a bit busy with the commentating and everything so I've not been out much to bars. I did have a lager in my hotel room last night, though, because I was really thirsty.

4. Favelas

The favelas are where the really poor people in Rio live, a bit like Moss Side but with better dancers than Bez, who some people say I look a bit like. We were advised not to go there as it's quite dangerous so I've not been there.

5. Sugarloaf Mountain

My favourite kind of loaf is the one with all the seeds in it that my wife gets, but you can't get that over here so I've not really had much toast since I've been here. From the top of Sugarloaf Mountain you can see the favelas and the Christ The Redeemer Statue and Copacabana Beach, where the temperature can sometimes be 25 degrees. Or 30.

2026 MONGO WORLD CUP TRIGGERS CONTROVERSY

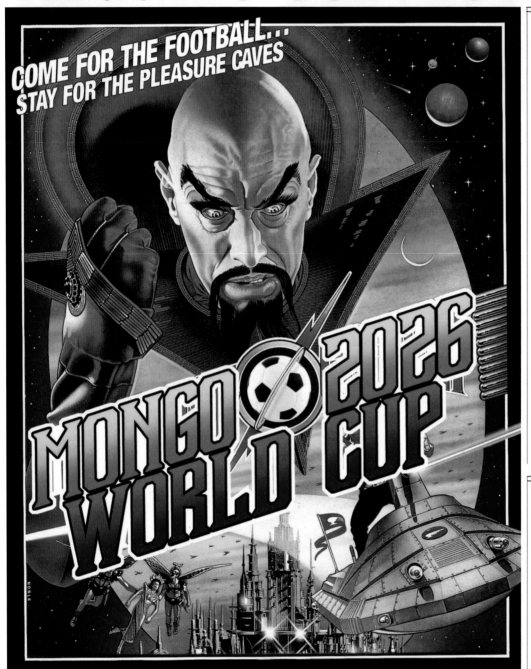

FIFA has promised an investigation into the successful 2026 World Cup bid by the planet Mongo.

Work on the stadia has been plagued with rumours that unions have been suppressed, worker wages withheld and the entire world is enslaved by the threat of an enormous death ray.

Ruler Ming The Merciless said: "Our bid was the most competitive and we're confident that the Hawkmen will be utterly crushed before the opening ceremony.

"The last thing anyone wants is Brian Blessed shouting abuse at the dancers and shitting on Pele from a height of 300 feet."

Reporter Dale Arden has managed to gain access to footage of Sepp Blatter having dinner with The Merciless in his palatial Magnetic Mountains residence while scantily-clad green women cavorted for their pleasure.

Documents also show that several high-ranking FIFA officials bought land in the uninhabitable Dire Marsh region before Mongo was named as host.

They have since made massive profits as the lands are drained to make way for infrastructure and by selling its native lizard men as meat.

Hull City to be renamed Hull Dildoes

HULL City owner Assem Allam plans a dildo-themed rebrand for the club, it has emerged.

After supporters rejected 'Hull Tigers' on the basis they are not an ice hockey team, the Hull Dildoes was suggested on the basis that the fans can go fuck themselves.

Allam said: "The new crest will be three gleaming synthetic dongs pointing heavenwards."

Supporters have opposed the move, arguing that a multimillionaire was not allowed to rename something they love just because he owns it.

Allam responded by renaming his family mansion 'Dr Pisswicket's House Of Pancakes' and his Rolls Royce 'The Egret Of Solitude'.

FA Cup won

THE FA Cup was won on Saturday.

The trophy was awarded to a football team at a London stadium and then kept in a cupboard overnight before being placed on a bus.

The FA Cup, known to some football aficionados as 'the cup', is contested over several rounds each year between many of England's teams.

The contest finishes each May with a match which can also be viewed on television.

Following the bus journey the trophy was placed in a cupboard made from glass. It may move to a different cupboard if the tournament is staged again.

How to vote for UKIP
page 27

Youngsters react to the pension crisis
page 31

Porking with John Snow
page 36

the daily mash

www.thedailymash.co.uk

RANDOM ACTS OF FOUL-MOUTHED CRUELTY

Monday 2015

Hideous Londoners forced to travel above ground

The twisted troglodytes who inhabit London have been forced to expose themselves to daylight.

THE near-blind, cannibalistic sub-humans, who usually live their short brutish lives in either tunnels or offices, are now groping their way through the capital's streets.

Nathan Muir, whose slimy green-white skin began to smoke and blossom into flame when touched by the sun, said: "The yellow eye in the heavens judges me.

"It burns me for my ugliness, because I defied the Lore by exposing my flesh to the Roofless World."

The stunted goblins are trained from birth never to make eye contact with one another and use their holy text *The Met Roe* to hide their faces.

Their subterranean world is paralysed by a vicious war between the Riders and the Drivers begun by the Drivers' megalomaniac leader, Crow.

Anthropologist Dr Helen Fisher said: "Crow demands an increase in tithe for the Drivers, insane idiot savants who spend their whole lives shackled to the controls of vast mechanical worms.

"Life is unimaginably awful down in the tunnels. There is a form of crude poetry inscribed on the walls, but it's not anything a normal human could enjoy."

FEATURE

Boudica's ...
Sideboobs of History

History is full of momentous side and underboob flashes – from Tamar seducing Judah in a roomy sarong right up to Lil' Kim coming out of the toilet in a pair of braces.

THE Druids' stubborn refusal to write anything down means that there is no contemporary record of my epic sideboob. But it was instrumental in how I inspired the people to follow me unquestioningly.

Sideboob looks easy, but is in fact a delicate operation requiring advanced understanding of the laws of physics. This is especially true for ladies with more than a handful, who will tend towards the more unpredictable 'shoogly sideboob'.

When I rode my horse through Anglesey at the start of my campaign, the hordes were on tenterhooks waiting for the bouncing motion to flop one right out of my billowing robes. But of course it didn't. This is because I'd craftily stuck my nipples onto the inside of the fabric with peat and spit, a technique later reinvented by **Anne Hathaway** at the 2006 Oscars. The confidence of a woman who marches without fear is what unites the masses behind her. Thus, Anne got an Academy award and all Welshmen will follow her into certain death.

Another technique used to great success in warfare is to write baffling Latin phrases up and down your sideboob. Nothing puts a Roman off his stroke more than some utter gibberish in his native tongue. I got inked with the phrase 'Repulsive cat ranger, rickets?' which made many a pillager furrow his brow just long enough for me to cleave his head in two with an axe.

The mighty warrior **Hayden Panettierre** is the greatest living advocate of this technique and, with her side boob etched with a load of old bollocks in Italian, continues to make Romans go boss-eyed well into the 21st century.

Anne Hathaway

Hayden Panettierre

LIDL LAUNCHES £12.99 TABLET

Budget supermarket Lidl has unveiled a tablet computer costing under thirteen pounds.

THE tablet, called the LiPad, has dispensed with an expensive touchscreen interface in favour of knobs which control the horizontal and vertical axes of a moveable cursor.

Users can draw their own entertainment on the screen, which uses magnetic aluminium technology.

A Lidl spokesman said: "The kids want a tablet, Granny wants a tablet, but we all know it'll be gathering dust in a cupboard in a month.

"With the LiPad you can still enjoy movies, games and surfing the web while exercising your imagination and creativity.

"For example, instead of boring old watching *Die Hard 4*, now you can create it yourself, frame-by-frame, then shake it away when you get bored."

Eight-year-old Tom Booker said: "I played with it for about 20 minutes, got bored, smashed it over my younger brother's head and broke the screen.

"Which is exactly what I would've done with an iPad Mini."

Tattoos must reflect owners' averageness

"I enjoy the music of Phil Collins"

TATTOO parlours must use designs that accurately reflect their recipients' mediocrity.

The new ruling was introduced after a bitter divorcee used Celtic-themed body art to pass himself off as a wild Pagan romantic.

Oriental lettering will be banned from people who have never been further east than Southend, and customers requesting a butterfly will have to go away and transform themselves into something beautiful first.

Nikki Hollis, from Peterborough, said: "I asked for 'What doesn't kill me makes me stronger' as I've always loved Professor Green's lyrics, but I ended up with 'I will die of natural causes aged around 82'.

"When I complained to the manager they offered to do another one for free but that one just said 'I really never learn, do I?' under a picture of a doughnut."

The most popular design – a dolphin – will be used only in exceptional circumstances for exceptional people and will generally be replaced by a battery hen to more accurately reflect the customer's lifestyle.

Existing tattoos will be allowed to remain as the older tiger, dragon and skull designs are gradually replaced by depictions of an open-plan call centre and parents not hugging their child enough.

Criticising schools 'vital' to shit parenting

Whatever they're doing, it's bad

CONSTANTLY criticising your child's school is a vital part of being a shit parent, it has been claimed.

Useless parents believe the best way to help their offspring is by reacting hysterically to anything the school does and regularly threatening to kick teachers' heads in.

Mother-of-two Emma Bradford said: "I found out the teachers at my son Callum's primary school had been making the children race each other for their own sick amusement.

"They dressed the kiddies up in little shorts and made it hard for them to run by making them carry an egg on a spoon. As well as the risk of paedophiles, the eggs are full of cholesterol.

"Callum was so traumatised he's not been able to do anything except steal bikes all week, so obviously I phoned the local paper."

Bradford added: "I went round to see the headmaster but he's still off work after I punched him for confiscating Callum's phone."

Parent Tom Logan said: "The teachers keep telling my kids all these terrifying stories about witches, transvestite wolves and this ravenous caterpillar that absolutely will not stop, like the fucking Terminator or something.

"It's no wonder they can't get to sleep after staying up till 3am drinking Coke and playing Need for Speed."

Jury asked if it could find Coulson 'ultra-guilty'

ANDY Coulson's completely obvious involvement in phone hacking prompted his trial jury to ask if they could find him more than guilty.

The former chief stalker at the *News of the World* was found guilty of conspiring to intercept phone messages after the judge turned down requests to find him 'super-guilty', 'ultra-guilty' and 'so-fucking-guilty'.

After resigning from the tabloid, Coulson became David Cameron's spin doctor because the Tory leader liked his dishonest face and his experience of working for an organisation that feasts on human souls.

A Downing Street spokesman said: "The prime minister is profoundly sorry that Andy got caught."

Meanwhile, the jury found Rebekah Brooks not guilty of phone hacking when she was *News of the World* editor, prompting experts to conclude that she must have been rubbish at her job.

Brooks and her husband Charlie are to launch a line of hand-stitched leather folders for concealing high-quality lesbian erotica.

So fucking guilty

Plans to spend more time with her idiot husband and his dirty pictures

Zuckerberg dies turning Facebook back on

MARK Zuckerberg has sacrificed himself to make Facebook work again.

After the social network went down, Zuckerberg led a team into the vast labyrinth of tunnels beneath Facebook HQ, discovering that to fix the problem one person would have to enter the website's radioactive core.

Facebook employee Tom Logan said: "Somehow a dead bird had gotten wedged between the nuclear-powered servers, triggering a meltdown.

"Mark knew doing the reboot was a one way journey. He refused a protective suit, as he was fully aware that it could not stop his organs liquefying.

"As the door slid shut behind him, he turned and gave a thumbs up through the hatch. It was the bravest thing I've ever seen."

FEATURE

Nigel Farage's guide to ...
Voting UKIP

Good morning and congratulations on making the best decision of your life – you're going to vote UKIP.

But how exactly do you do that? Is it true that UKIP are so outside the political system that you can register your vote by making a deliciously politically incorrect remark in a public place?

Sadly not, though don't let that stop you. Just follow the steps below:

● Head out to your local polling station, but be wary. Primary schools are hotbeds of trendy liberal Marxism, and that wall display could be multicultural propaganda.

● Dress smartly to act as an ambassador for your party. Men should wear a blazer, tie and biscuit-coloured trousers. Women should be well-groomed and not vote.

● Do not be tempted by false UKIPs like an Independence From Europe, No2EU and the English Democrats. They are serpents sent to sway you from the path of righteousness.

● Make your cross in the box next to your local UKIP candidate's name. Don't worry if you don't recognise it – he'll soon be on the TV news for saying things about gays.

● Don't add another four lines to your cross to make a cheeky little swastika. This counts as spoiling your ballot and is a major reason why right-wing parties underperform in elections.

● Finally, enjoy yourself! Take your time, drink in the surroundings and savour the moment. After all, you're never going to vote UKIP again.

Britain is being inundated with accusations of racism. Take our quick test to find out how much you dislike others on the basis of ethnicity.

ARE YOU A RACIST?

1. Do you think all Romanians are thieves?
   a) No, I don't.
   b) Not *all* of them, no.
   c) Of course, that's why they're all so swarthy.

2. Have you ever tried to scare people with false claims about Eastern European immigration?
   a) No, I haven't.
   b) Yes, but only because I'm weak willed and eager to please.
   c) It's pretty much how I spend my day.

3. Do you think people who make horrible generalisations about Muslims are 'idiots'?
   a) Yes, but I also think they're horribly racist.
   b) Yes, but I'm just saying that to sound vaguely reasonable.
   c) Yes, they should only say that sort of thing in a private meeting.

4. Have you ever used the term 'EUSSR'?
   a) No, not even when expressing my disdain for people who use the term 'EUSSR'.
   b) Yes, but only when expressing my disdain for people who use the term 'EUSSR'.
   c) I use it all the time.

5. Do you think there is something intrinsically virtuous about being 'Anglo Saxon'?
   a) No, I actually find the whole thing rather embarrassing.
   b) No, it's much the same as being French, but without all the fucked-up geese.
   c) Saying the words 'Anglo Saxon' makes me climax.

So, are you a racist?

Mostly 'a': You're probably not racist, but it was only five questions and for all we know you may have an irrational hatred of the Dutch.

Mostly 'b': You're a bit racist, mostly when reading certain newspapers. And you can stop any time you want, by the way.

Mostly 'c': You're a racist even though you say you're not and you get all offended by the very idea, like the racist you obviously are.

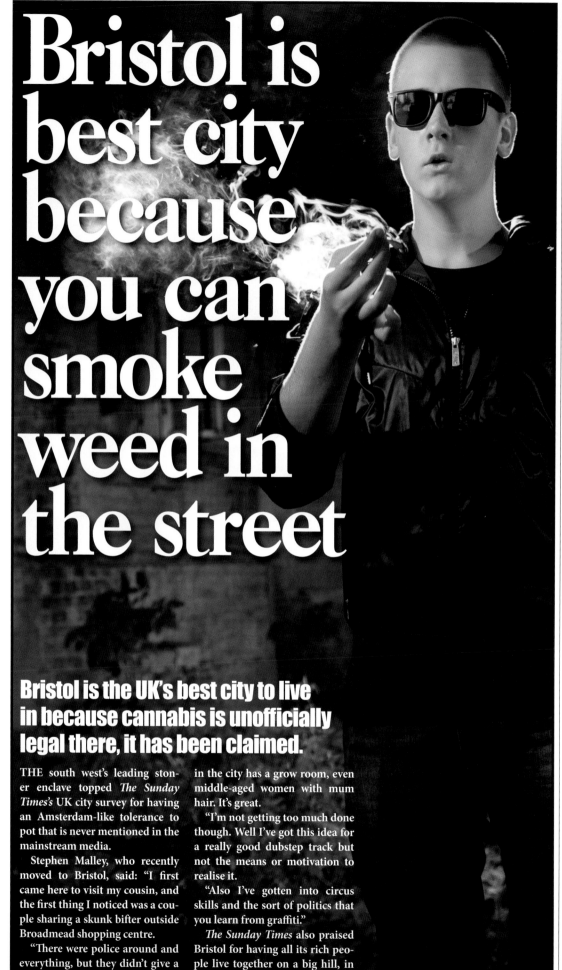

Bristol is best city because you can smoke weed in the street

Bristol is the UK's best city to live in because cannabis is unofficially legal there, it has been claimed.

THE south west's leading stoner enclave topped *The Sunday Times's* UK city survey for having an Amsterdam-like tolerance to pot that is never mentioned in the mainstream media.

Stephen Malley, who recently moved to Bristol, said: "I first came here to visit my cousin, and the first thing I noticed was a couple sharing a skunk bifter outside Broadmead shopping centre.

"There were police around and everything, but they didn't give a toss.

"Since moving down I've discovered that every other person in the city has a grow room, even middle-aged women with mum hair. It's great.

"I'm not getting too much done though. Well I've got this idea for a really good dubstep track but not the means or motivation to realise it.

"Also I've gotten into circus skills and the sort of politics that you learn from graffiti."

The Sunday Times also praised Bristol for having all its rich people live together on a big hill, in a weird kind of segregation that gives it "an interesting science fiction feel".

Also there are good schools and shit like that

Things cannot be dumbed down any further, warn experts

CULTURE is reaching a point of maximum dumbness, it has been claimed.

Researchers at the Institute for Studies have warned that it will soon be impossible to dumb down news and entertainment media any further.

Professor Henry Brubaker said: "Most television is about cooking, the paranormal or poor people having arguments. The news is just opinions punctuated with pictures of 'extreme weather'.

"The only books being published are ghost-written celebrity biographies or thrillers about serial killers called things like 'The Face Collector'. Apart from that people just read lists of '10 facts about muscle growth' off websites.

"The problem is that although our culture cannot get any stupider, human intelligence may continue on its downward trajectory.

"The result will be a world in which nobody understands anything. Even a film about The Rock driving a jeep into explosions will leave viewers confused and angry at its pretentiousness."

However TV channel boss Mary Fisher said: "Don't worry, I've just commissioned *Jamie & Jimmy's Paranormal Antiques Auction Sex News.*"

Speak Foreign with Farage
Available in Bloody French,
Bloody German, and Bloody Spanish.

Special sections on talking common sense, asking
for a proper English ale and claiming huge expenses.

YOUNG PEOPLE JUST GOING TO CHANGE PENSION AGE BACK LATER

Young people have announced plans to lower the pension age by several decades once they are in charge.

WHEN asked how they felt about working for another 45 years before getting a state pension, all under-25s favoured amending the law as soon as those who made it get old and feeble.

Nail artist Emma Bradford, aged 19, said: "I have to retire at 70 to pay for my granny to retire at 62? Yeah, sounds perfectly fair to me.

"Or here's another plan: how about we wait until all the government are dead, then just switch it back?"

Tom Logan, a 22-year-old trainee lawyer, said: "This government telling us what's going to be happening in 2063 is like a mayfly making big plans for next month.

"So if they're in power until 2020 at the latest, and me and my mates get into government in 2040, that still gives us what, 20 years to change that back?

"Pretty sure we'll manage it. It'll be our second priority after legalising euthanasia."

Treasury Secretary Danny Alexander said: "We cannot ignore the deficit, so the only responsible thing to do is to leave all our unpaid bills for young people who can't get jobs.

"There is a slight risk that, when they've got all the money and power, the younger generation may act in their own selfish interest."

Will overpower a 78-year-old George Osborne

Women 'should be banned'

WOMEN are too much trouble and should be banned, UKIP leader Nigel Farage has claimed.

After commenting that women who had children were less valuable employees for City firms, Farage said he had now come to the conclusion that women are just a nuisance in general.

Farage said: "Having children is incredibly stressful for employers and women should stop doing it, or not get a job in the first place and stay at home baking cakes and lactating.

"However, women are a lot of hassle in many other ways. They clutter up the bathroom, weep all the time and want to talk about feelings instead of cricket.

"And of course you waste an awful lot of time having sex with them or helping them reverse park, when you could be running a political party to stop Britain losing its sovereignty to unelected EU bureaucrats.

"I'm not suggesting we put them in prison or anything like that, just special knitting camps."

Teacher Tom Logan said: "I'm not bitter about my three failed marriages, however it's obvious to me that women are highly desirable yet also evil. Basically they are succubi.

"We could all do with a break from them. Then we could throw ourselves into untroubling male activities like fishing and visiting tool shops."

Look at them gossiping

Buy the food, or

no more breasts

MARKS &

FEATURE

The Daily Mash Guide to ...
Internet Passwords

The password to all your money is probably your surname or dog's name with '01' after it.

Most Britons lack the tiny amount of imagination required to think up a credible password. Here's the Daily Mash guide to protecting your cyber-assets:

- It's too easy to guess a password if it's the name of something you love, like your partner or your favourite sandwich. Instead use as your password something that you fucking hate, like your ex-partner or his dog that you ran over.

- If you must use something you love, choose something that nobody knows about your passion for, like your favourite actor in early 90s erotic thrillers. Actually, that's perfect. Everyone just use Shannon Tweed.

- Instead of using an easily guessable string of numbers like 123456, use something complicated and difficult to work out, like the square root of 15,241,383,936.

- Alternatively 5318008 upside-down on a calculator spells BOOBIES.

- The most secure passwords are mnemonics, where the initial letters of a phrase spell it out. "Prince Acting Super-Sexy Won't Orally Reciprocate, Damn" is a pretty unbreakable one.

- Choose a nine-letter word, jumble it up, and replace four of the letters with numbers that multiplied together make 334. Although this won't stop Rachel Riley off *Countdown*'s persistent attempts to hack your Gmail account.

Children naturally awful

Kids are dreadful regardless of whether they've had sugar, it has emerged.

THE Institute for Studies monitored the behaviour of a group of under-tens before and after eating an immense bag of Haribo Star Mix.

Professor Henry Brubaker said: "They were little fuckers before eating the sweets and they were little fuckers after. Basically they're little fuckers.

"The effect of sugar has long been exaggerated by parents keen to refute the obvious truth that their offspring are drooling, messy little psychopaths whose main goal is finding animals to harm."

Seven-year-old Emma Bradford, who had not eaten anything sugary, said: "I hit Gerald in the face for no reason."

Then she pointed to a table and asked "What's that?" 28 times before deliberately running face first into a door and blaming someone else.

Professor Brubaker said: "Sugar does virtually nothing. I just had a cup of tea with four sugars in it and it's not like I've done an E. Everything is normal.

"Clearly there are chemicals that would affect kids' behaviour. Really strong sedatives that make them into docile zombies, devoid of the spark and spontaneity of youth.

"There may be some people who see that as a bad thing."

Pretty girl in summer dress is most depressing sight imaginable

AN attractive young woman in a pretty summer dress is putting men and women alike in a terrible mood.

The unidentified pretty girl was described by onlookers as having an utterly carefree manner. She exuded youth, beauty and an innocent sensuality.

36-year-old Tom Logan said: "She was like a lovely living statue or some nymph from Welsh mythology, a beautiful mystical thing.

"However I am tired, old and miserable. She would rather die than glance at me.

"I hate myself and my tired lust."

Office worker Emma Bradford said: "I love her dress but I would definitely look a bit fat in it.

"By comparison I am a massive, sweaty sow. To hell with everything, I'm going to buy the biggest possible bag of Haribo and consume it in the toilet at work."

Father-of-two Stephen Malley said: "I love my family but part of me now wants to abandon them. Summer is such a downer."

FEATURE

Jon Snow's ...
Can I Pork That?

Whenever any object enters my field of vision my first thought is, can I have sex with it? I'll admit my enthusiasm for physical love of all stripes has caused awkward situations over the years, not least when I chased Alex Ferguson round and round the C4 studio à la The Benny Hill Show.

Based on personal experience, here's my expert advice on a few things you may be considering doing it with.

● **Angela Merkel**

Angela exudes the distinctive musk of the alpha female. I'd describe her scent as fried peaches with overtones of the forest. And like a forest she is both alluring and fraught with hidden danger.

● **Compost bin**

I call mine Renee. I clamber into her, and we are joined in mulchy union. Note: however many times you ask, Angela Merkel will not get into a compost bin with you, she's just not into it and actually gets quite snarly if you persist.

● **Acoustic guitar**

I have sex with it then I play it then I have sex with it and then I play it. Everybody's happy. Especially the audience.

● **Avocados**

Its confident Latin heritage and abundant folic acid makes the avocado not only a superb sexual comrade-in-arms but also an excellent mate for the production of offspring.

● **A Blu-Ray disc of Zero Dark Thirty**

I enjoyed this film so much, I simply had to ask it out for dinner. I didn't know if I would want to have sex with it, but I did and it was every bit as thrilling and fraught with danger as the mission to assassinate Osama Bin Laden.

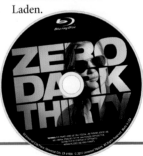

FEATURE

- ### Mediocre framed watercolour of a dog
  My wife was like, 'What the hell are you doing with that picture, we've got guests!' I explained that I wasn't into dogs, it was the texture of the canvas that got me all fizzed up. However she said I had to get a replacement, £400 gone just like that.

- ### Praying mantis
  Those big eyes and sensual feelers say 'yes' but the sharp mandibles and armoured appendages say 'no'. I definitely regretted this one, although on similar insect lines I did enjoy a great five-way with some locusts in Uganda.

- ### Desk
  The rectangularity of desks really turns me on. However like many items of furniture they can be frustratingly short on 'access points'. You need one of those old school desks with an inkwell.

JESUS DIED TO GIVE US TWO BANK HOLIDAYS

The Archbishop of Canterbury has given thanks to Jesus, who gave his life so that we could have not just a Monday off work but a Friday too.

JESUS, God's only begotten son, died for his belief that workers deserve a four-day paid break just when the weather's beginning to pick up.

Archbishop Justin Welby said: "The heavenly miracle of Good Friday was bought with the blood of the Lamb, spilt for everyone who's got a bit of decorating to do.

"How can the atheists scoff when only eight days of leave need be booked to give sixteen days off? Marvel at the ways of the Lord."

Biblical scholars say that Jesus was a carpenter, hard at work in Nazareth, before he received a divine revelation telling him to take a few days off and maybe catch some rays at the Sea of Galilee.

Jesus's teachings spread until Easter became a holiday long enough to get 12 mates together and head into Jerusalem for a big meal with plenty of wine.

The Archbishop, reading from the Bible, said: "Now when the evening did come, He died on the cross. And behold, on the third day He rose again nice and late after his first proper lie-in in ages.

"And He said unto them, Fear not ye for there is still no work tomorrow. Lo, does anyone fancy an afternoon session?"

Children of hippy parents getting shit eggs again

HIPPY parents will be giving their children drab, joyless dairy-free Easter eggs again this year, it has been confirmed.

As the egg rush begins, middle class eco-parents confirmed plans to disappoint their offspring with bland healthy eggs in unexciting boxes.

Mother-of-two Emma Bradford said: "Despite their pleading, I don't want my children being indoctrinated by the corporate chocolate behemoth.

"A Crunchie bar is a chocolate-covered phallic symbol laden with carcinogens, while I've read on parenting forums that Cadbury's Creme Eggs are the product of grotesque genetic engineering where fondant is injected into hens.

"I shall be visiting my local independent wholefoods store and getting two NatureForest Gluten-Free Carob Ovals. Or maybe some Earth's Way Non-Denominational Mini Planets.

"They come in tasteful packaging with pastoral imagery and cost about twenty pounds each, not that you can put a price on being a good person."

Bradford's seven-year-old son Tom said: "I'm never allowed anything fun.

"But that's ok, I'll just wait until I grow up then unleash my pent-up urges on drugs and alcohol."

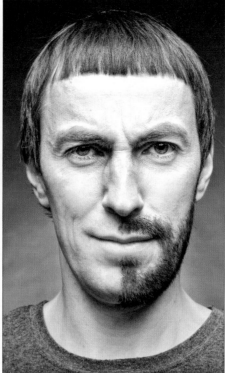

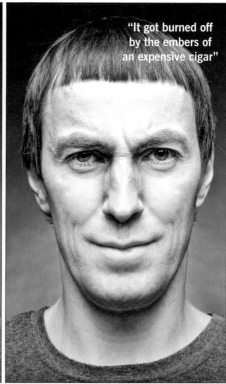

"It got burned off by the embers of an expensive cigar"

Men seeking plausible beard exit strategies

Millions of men are about to pretend a shaving accident caused them to remove their beard.

AFTER the UK reached beard saturation point when one of Boyzone got one, men are desperate to remove their facial hair without appearing to be weak-willed fashion victims.

Tom Logan, 31, from Hatfield, said: "I was making some toast, the tip of my beard went in the toaster, suddenly it was on fire and I had to cut it all off.

"Total accident. I would not be so feeble as to substantially alter my appearance because of an article in the *Guardian*.

"I mean for fuck's sake, I'm a man."

Graphic designer Stephen Malley, 29, said: "The reason for my new clean-shaven look is that I went to get a passport photo done and you aren't allowed facial hair because of anti-terrorism laws."

Wayne Hayes, 33, from Stevenage, said: "Mine got stuck in a door, it was a case of pull it out by the roots or starve to death.

"As an unreconstructed alpha male who doesn't give a shit about media-driven style trends and is basically a raw sexy ape I chose the former, but purely for survival reasons.

"Then I applied moisturiser to the affected area."

Students home to dump boyfriends and fix parents' broadband

THE UK's students have arrived home to get their parents' internet working and end long-term relationships.

Students surveyed have admitted they are not looking forward to either task, though are divided about which will prove more onerous.

Carolyn Ryan, studying French at Keele, said: "The broadband, which hasn't worked since November with the bonus of really unclut-

tering my Facebook feed, is probably going to be a matter of turning it off and on again.

"The boyfriend, on the other hand, needs to be gently told that it's over without arousing suspicion that I've been shagging our corridor's Resident Advisor since the second day of term."

Biochemistry student, Nathan Muir, said: "The PC at home's going to be a four-hour job, because Dad has no idea how to clear the viruses

and spyware from all the porn sites he pretends he doesn't visit.

"Breaking up with Megan, on the other hand, should be as easy as showing her my new rainbow flag and 'I Heart Boys' tattoos."

Students have confirmed that once those unpleasant jobs are disposed of, they will be clogging up pubs to show off their new piercings while having loud conversations about structured oppression.

British men in Barcelona shirts hoping you'll ask

THE PUBLIC has been warned not to approach men wearing Barcelona shirts who clearly have no ethnic affiliation to the Catalan region.

The men, usually aged between 25 and 50, are rated a category five risk of telling you at length why they personally identify with the continental model of play.

Inspector Tom Booker said: "Men in Barcelona shirts believe that their sartorial choice associates them with the insouciant, free-passing artfulness that has conquered an era. It's extremely unpleasant."

Nathan Muir, wearing a Xavi top, said: "Building slowly from the back, being calm and precise in the middle and finishing with dazzling flair is, coincidentally, how I make love to women."

New Scotland kit reflects country's tradition of twee indie music

Scotland's new away kit represents the country's history of producing delicate indie music for manchildren, according to the SFA.

THE strip was launched on Wednesday to a fanfare of jangly guitars and a maudlin rendition of *Lloyd, I'm Ready To Be Heartbroken* by Camera Obscura.

As well as a pink and yellow hooped shirt and socks, Scottish players will also be issued with an anorak, a pair of thick-rimmed glasses held together with Sellotape, and a dream journal.

An SFA spokesman said: "From the Pastels to BMX Bandits to Belle & Sebastian, Scotland has long been a global leader in wistful disappointment, thanks to our natural abundance of sexless, pasty-faced introverts.

"This kit stands for being obsessed with a girl who doesn't know you exist, walking through the rain feeling melancholy but strangely uplifted, and writing excruciating love poetry well into your twenties.

"It's just what you'd expect from the nation that gave the world Teenage Fanclub, Dogs Die In Hot Cars, and Pat Nevin."

The shirt, available in all sizes from S to XXXS, is made from high-tech microfibres that absorb, reflect and magnify the wearer's crippling self-doubt.

They're a team but also lonely

Fan fury as footballer looks up while being abused

THE Football Supporters' Association has complained after a player made eye contact during a chant about his whore mother.

Fan Tom Logan said: "It is simply irresponsible for a highly-paid professional to taunt fans by deliberately hearing accusations that his mum does it for fags with sailors.

"By casting his eyes across the crowd he as good as tore up those seats and threw them at police himself, and should be charged accordingly."

The controversial glance follows an incident where a top-level player was hit by a sharpened coin and blatantly displayed his bleeding wound to the crowd, for which he was fined £265,000 and banned for three games.

An FSA spokesman said: "Footballers earn millions of pounds every year from us, the fans. In return, all we ask is that they play brilliantly, never go out, remain utterly loyal until unceremoniously ditched, be perfect role models and soak up all the abuse that we throw at them. And their wives. And their pets."

And there's the enticing tang of raw sewage

UK surfers prepare for summer of living in wrong country

Britain's surfers are ready for the summer season during which they might surf as many as five times.

THE surfers, who can be identified by their surf clothes, surfboard roof racks and the surf stickers on their cars, are excited about the 12 to 24 breakers they will spend upward of 120 hours catching this year.

Wayne Hayes of Derby said: "Your boy here was born to ride the waves.

"Every fourth weekend I spend 10 hours driving to Cornwall, then another two hours queuing to get to the beach, then four hours in the water waiting for a good spot before I get my surf on.

"Providing the weather doesn't turn, of course."

Hayes, who describes himself as an archetypal surfer dude, has a model VW camper van on his desk at work, regularly watches *Point Break* and owns six wetsuits.

He is one of thousands of British surfers who spend less than 0.9 per cent of each year taking part in the activity around which their identities are constructed.

Professional surfer Stephen Malley said:

"Surfing was invented in Hawaii, a place of year-round sunshine and big waves, and popularised in California where again, sunshine and waves.

"Here in Britain there are about seven beaches that get big waves, mainly in October and November when the water's so cold it makes your balls permanently retract.

"Technically it's surfing. Technically a Robin Reliant is a motorbike."

Stephen Hendry to go outside

SNOOKER legend Stephen Hendry has revealed plans to venture outdoors for the first time in his adult life.

The seven-time world champion was raised by umpires after being abandoned as a baby on the fire escape of a snooker hall.

Since then he used underground sewer tunnels to travel between match venues before finally retiring to a makeshift dwelling underneath a snooker table.

"The snooker authorities tell me I have earned my freedom. Now I may go beyond the doors, where I understand my winnings can be exchanged for clothes, food and even a house."

Hendry admitted feeling a mixture of excitement and trepidation about his planned venture into 'Skyland': "They say the sky is as blue as the blue ball and fields as green as the green ball. A floor not coated in a dull grey carpet but with a material called 'stone'.

"I am especially interested to discover flowers, which I understand smell of something other than decades-old cigarette smoke."

One of these is right

Clocks go either back or forward this weekend or next weekend

The UK has been reminded that the clocks go forward for spring, or possibly back, this Saturday or maybe the Saturday after.

THE BIANNUAL ritual, which corrects time for the benefit of the ever-grateful farming community, will give everyone an extra hour in bed, if it's not an hour less.

A spokesman for Greenwich Royal Observatory said: "Frankly we're sketchy on the specifics.

"You think we're a bunch of people who look like Kraftwerk, sitting in a clock-covered spaceship thing that is calibrated to the last nano-second.

"Actually it's a rented room above Greenwich Wetherspoons and we drink heavily through boredom.

"We advise boozing a lot on Saturday evening to avoid the jarring sensation of time dislocation, ideally blacking out before 1am.

"Wait until you're properly pissed before changing the clocks. Use the al-ternating method – one forward then one backward and don't be afraid to do the same clock twice.

"Set the telly to ITV+1 so you're not spun out when you wake up, and if any device updates its own time it is the devil's tool and should be smashed with a hammer.

"But it's all up to you really, do what you want."

Babies cry out of spite

INFANTS cry at night because they're little bastards, according to new research.

Cameras in nurseries showed that babies timed their bawling to coincide with parents opening a bottle of wine or initiating sexual intercourse for the first time in three months.

Eight-month-old Kyle Stephenson said: "I'm perfectly capable of going to the toilet myself but just enjoy the disgusted look on their stupid faces when they're dealing with my pungent bodily waste."

Professor Henry Brubaker of the Institute For Studies said: "We asked parents to point at their crying baby and say 'Enough of this shit, I know your game and it won't work'. 90 per cent of the time the infant would simply shrug and go back to sleep.

"Some of them even left a note in their cot the following morning, apologising for being a little tosser."

But Stephenson warned: "I think I can feel a tooth coming through so they should probably bin that *House of Cards* box set."

thedailymash

www.thedailymash.co.uk　　**RANDOM ACTS OF FOUL-MOUTHED CRUELTY**　　Monday 2015

PUBS TO TRIAL PROFESSIONAL LANES

Britain's pubs will have a section of the bar reserved for people who know what they're doing this Christmas.

WITH Christmas hostelries full of people buying coffee with a debit card, sections of the bar will be solely for habitual drinkers who want to get hammered and know precisely how they'd like that to happen.

Pub owner Tom Logan said: "While I'm giving samples of our real ale to some bell-end who's just going to order a half of Fosters, I could be servicing our core clientele of red men with poor home lives.

"Christmas is a time for happiness, family and laughter so I should be getting our regulars – who have none of those things – as pissed as possible."

Users of the professional lane require a drinker's licence. Applicants are assessed on whether they order Guinness before their other drinks, can demonstrate awareness of how long others have been waiting and are able to carry three drinks without a tray.

Pub aficionado Wayne Hayes said: "My local has the misfortune of being bang opposite the business district so every December I'm forced to wait an extra 90 seconds to self-medicate with Stella while some lightweight goes through the crisp options for the fourth time.

"Roll on January when the only sound to be heard in here is the gentle sobbing of Frank after his horse comes in fifth."

WHO IS THE NEW HITLER?

Which of Europe's powerful freaks is the real heir to the Great Dictator?

Boggle-eyed xenophobes are seizing power across the continent. But which one could fill Adolf Hitler's jackboots?

1. Marine Le Pen

French National Front leader whose name means 'The Pen by the Sea', which she hopes to fill with people who don't eat pig's testicles. Le Pen is looking for a way to conquer Europe with an army that demands four-hour lunch breaks.
Odds of being new Hitler: **5/1**

2. Morten Messerschmidt

The great-grandson of a Luftwaffe Messerschmitt 109 plane which was forced down in Copenhagen during WWII and fell in love with a farm girl, this propeller-driven Danish leader believes in closing borders, cutting benefits and an 80 per cent increase in Lego Nazi play sets.
Odds of being new Hitler: **18/1**

3. Nigel Farage

UKIP leader considered charismatic in Britain but viewed by Europeans roughly as we view Ed Miliband. Credibility with military low after his 2010 election day attempt at piloting a light aircraft in a bombing run on Buckingham ended in disaster.
Odds of being new Hitler: **100/1**

4. Adolf Hitler

Former German Chancellor now in present day after a failed assassination attempt by the inventor of a time machine. Currently building support in German beer halls, the all-new Hitler has swept away doubters with his fashionable quiff and handlebar moustache.
Odds of being new Hitler: **Evens**

UK thanks Russell Brand

THAT not-voting thing has worked out brilliantly, Britain has told Russell Brand.

33-year-old Wayne Hayes said: "I really stuck it to The Man by staying at home on Thursday, even if it does look an awful lot like The Man ended up succeeding beyond his wildest imaginings."

As two-thirds of the electorate decided not to bother in the European election, the UK will now be represented in Brussels by MEPs who won't bother voting either.

The long-term plan is for all political decisions to be made in a Mayfair drinking club without the costly and time-consuming exercise of pretending to care less what the public thinks.

Jester/prophet/lothario/voice of cinema rabbit Russell Brand said: "Cor, it's a proper xenophobey-wobey paradigm shift toward the far righty-wight malarkey, innit?

"How very un-perspicacious of me 'umble self to not divine how this whole politics imbroglio might have unfolded."

Caffè Italiano

It
Moves
My
Bowels

The perfect beans,
the perfect blend,
the perfect start

The Marquis de Sade's Guide to Curling

I – A Story of Ice

As you already know, dear reader, all ice in the land is the property of a certain Lord C__, who demands that it be polished to such a state that he may toss items down it with precision.

A set of scrubbing girls, handpicked by Lord C__, are employed in the discipline of preparing the ice just the way he likes it.

II – A Story of Stone

Our chief scrubber, with arms as robust and hairy as a man's thigh and eyes which constantly scream at one another for help, launches the massive shiny stone across the rink and shrieks directions in a language only it can understand.

But there is so much spittle frothing around her cavernous mouth that the stone is getting confused and veering wildly off course. The other scrubbers, who collectively boast three brooms and six jolly buttocks (but sadly cannot count past number eleven) are madly buffing every inch of ice as Lord C__ looks down on them with disgust.

III – A Story of Blood

The flag goes up for the gravest offense in curling: in her excitement, one of the scrubbers has done a little wee on the ice. Mayhem ensues. Our esteemed friends, Jane T__ and Christopher D__, invade the rink in an effort to lay down the law.

But alas they're not as young as once they were: Mr D__ stumbles backwards, impaling himself onto the blade of Ms T__'s skate (dear reader, in the most unfortunate way). Many a young man has perished on the end of Ms T__'s blade, but Christopher D__ is an iceman of some experience and remains impressively buoyant. The pair, unable to disconnect, rise up like an unstoppable, nightmarish chimera. To rapturous applause, the blood-drenched beast begins victory laps, waving and punching the air.

King Herod's...
Family Christmas

I once had a Christmas when my scrotum rotted and dropped off, plunging me into several days of agonised madness.

However, this was a picnic compared to most years. Who among us can genuinely say they haven't spent at least one Christmas hysterically screaming for the executions of their own families and thousands of others?

Take my mother, Cyprus the Nabataean. Like most mums this time of year, she refuses to move for the duration of the day and expects every relation from miles around to make the pilgrimage to her, like she's the Blarney Stone or something.

Then there's her new partner. I used to breed rhinos back in Galilee and this is exactly what it's like dealing with him. Just when you think it's safe to let a new male mingle with the herd, he goes on a mental rampage for no reason whatsoever. It will only end after he's speared another adult male with his massive horn and you've placated him with a bottle of Corona and *Finding Nemo* on Sky Movies.

My brother's girlfriend, Salome, used to liven up every yuletide. A proper good time girl – no one'll ever forget the dance she did at my birthday party, least of all John the Baptist. But since she's had a baby all that is history. Now it's like inviting Mariah Carey: she brings her own bottled water with her because my tap water's not good enough for her anymore and goes in a huff if you don't have any of her bullshit herbal tea. Then, she needs her 'quiet room' for breastfeeding. It's not like there's anyone here who hasn't seen them a hundred times before. Anyway, she's full of crap: I listened at the door and she was playing Candy Crush for 45 minutes.

In these circumstances it is understandable how someone may end up ordering a few mass killings. I don't remember saying that, but then again I was very upset. It does sound like the kind of thing I might say and my scribes agreed I definitely said it. Point is: everyone's said things in the heat of the moment at this time of year.

My advice would be to execute all your scribes and then hire some new ones after you've had a Bellini and are feeling a little more magnanimous.

It is a sad thing

JORDAN VERY SAD

Jordan is sad now because she got married to a man but he is a bad man.

JORDAN is in the paper and on telly too sometimes but not so much these days. She has big boobs and a big house, like what you want.

She said: "I am sad, the man is bad and he did a thing that made me feel upset inside.

"I want to go in my house and cry. He is a dirty, dirty man.

"I want a man to be nice to me, then I will not be sad. I will be happy."

The reason Jordan is sad is that the man put it in a woman, like when a man and woman make a baby but not like that because they do not love each other.

The man said: "I am a bad man. I liked doing the thing with the lady when I did it, but now I think it was not a good idea."

Jordan wrote on the Twitter: "All of the men just think about putting it in many women. Why is this?

"I like horses."

38-year-old *Heat* reader Mary Fisher said: "The man is bad. I want Jordan to go on a horse with Peter Andre.

"The horse has wings and they will fly up in the sky forever."

Harry and Cressida split after she stumbles across 'The Room'

PRINCE Harry has split from girlfriend Cressida Bonas after she accidentally entered the special room at Kensington Palace.

Friends say the split is amicable, but it is understood the young socialite is currently at a secret location in Hampshire and will take at least three years to return to normal.

A source said: "They were having a lovely time together. They would snuggle and laugh but then Harry's expression would change very suddenly and he would say 'do not enter the room'.

"Cressie had no intention of doing so, but she woke up in the middle of the night and went for a wander until she came to a door, behind which she could hear cruel laughter and a terrified voice pleading 'no, no, no'.

"She opened the door to see all of them – including that Autumn Phillips – pointing crossbows at a naked little Welshman standing on a bucket.

"She screamed, they turned and stared at her and then two Grenadier Guards appeared from nowhere and injected her in the forehead with a potent sedative."

The source added: "It's a shame because they would have made such a perfect couple if she'd been willing to take part in the rituals."

FOREIGN AID SHOULD BE SPENT ON REPLACING BRITISH CARPETS

45p

pill for every reader

For the love of God, can we at least get some samples to those most in need?

The *Daily Mail* has called on the government to stop sending money to poor foreigners when it could be used to replace carpets right here in Britain.

THE newspaper has launched a petition which has actually been signed by people.

In a hard-hitting editorial the paper said that British carpets must always come first and that most foreign aid was used to build Chinese spaceships.

Meanwhile, the *Mail* underlined the horrifying extent of Britain's humanitarian crisis by illustrating its story with a photo of a moist BMW.

Martin Bishop, from Somerset, said: "I've only had this carpet six months and now it's all soggy. I'm really unhappy, but the government won't even buy me a new telly."

His wife Sarah added: "How many BMWs have to get wet before the government stops trying to impress stupid African babies?"

Professor Henry Brubaker, from the Institute for Studies, said: "People who don't have flood insurance either didn't ask for it, which is mentally defective, or were denied it, which should have caused the first faint stirrings of something being amiss.

"If we are going to use some foreign aid money, perhaps we could make a film about how not to buy a house on a flood plain.

"It'll be called *How Not to Buy a House on a Flood Plain*, it will be 10 seconds long and consist of me holding up a piece of cardboard on which I will have written 'don't buy a house on a flood plain.' "

He added: "Meanwhile, you can still do your bit for Britain. If you meet someone today who has signed the Mail's petition, try your very best to urinate on their legs."

The heartbreaking moment Mail Online journalist realised his soul had died

THIS picture shows the very moment at which a journalist discovered he had died inside.

38-year-old *Mail Online* staffer Wayne Haynes had just uploaded a picture of some grieving relatives to his employer's website.

He said: "At that precise second, I knew I was not a man but a ghoul. A professional 'grief pinpointer' for whom human misery is a form of light entertainment to be sandwiched between adverts for chocolate and women's tops.

"I had left humanity via a one-way exit.

"I'm just glad someone was there with a camera, so that they could take a picture and put it on to the internet."

Mail sacks Dacre, hires de Botton

THE *Daily Mail* has sacked long-time editor Paul Dacre and replaced him with the philosopher Alain de Botton.

Owner, Viscount Rothermere, said: "I read Alan's website, the *Philosophers' Mail*, and just loved  it. Alain is a gentle, thoughtful human, whereas Paul Dacre's a lunatic who frightens me each and every day.

"Alan will turn the *Daily Mail* into something wise and beautiful that radiates truth, intelligence and, most importantly, love.

"And, best of all, Alain doesn't want any money. He just wants five minutes a day to look at a tree.

"Unlike Dacre, who is a greedy bastard."

Bangladeshi house slave

"Why waste more time on boring trips to Primark and Topshop when you can hire Amina, 15, to make all your clothes for 13p a day."

The perfect gift for Mother's Day

'LONDON TWAT DRAIN' GREAT FOR PROVINCES

Provincial cities have hailed the capital's boom in knobhead jobs as the best thing that's ever happened to them.

WITH more than 80% of new jobs for complete tools being created in London, cities like Manchester and Newcastle are seeing record levels of twat migration.

Professor Henry Brubaker of the Institute for Studies said: "London has now passed what we call the Twat Event Horizon.

"Put simply, once a core number of self-involved wankers is reached then the city becomes as irresistibly attractive to twats as it is repellent to everyone else. Thereafter, their numbers grow exponentially.

"More than 85 per cent of people now living in London are twats."

Shipworker Norman Steele said: "My son, who has an ironic basin haircut, moved to London because there weren't any design agencies with ping-pong tables here in Sunderland.

"He says he'd love to visit but he can't spend 24 hours anywhere without a vibrant DIY chill-wave scene. It's great."

Mayor of Leeds Roy Hobbs said: "I walk the streets of my city, denuded as they are of dicks, wankers, and shameless cocksticks, and I feel proud.

"We don't need organic vegetables or truffle oil or quinoa anymore, so there's more room in the shops for Toffos and Vimto and HP Sauce.

"Nightclubs are, by law, called either the Ritz or Zanzibar and are explicitly for getting drunk, dancing to happy hardcore and getting off with birds.

"In this land of dark satanic mills we have built a paradise."

"Back home they used to call me a bell-end"

Lent 'bollocks'

LENT is bollocks, it has been confirmed.

As millions began a six-week period of self-denial, experts stressed it was stupid and wrong.

Professor Henry Brubaker, from the Institute for Studies, said: "Maybe you think self-denial is 'good for the soul'. Try saying that out loud.

"Or perhaps you think it will make you live longer in which case your skull is so full of bollocks they're coming out of your nose.

"But I suspect you're really doing it to provide yet another opening gambit for one of your 'conversations'.

"So, in summary, shut up about Lent. You idiots."

NORTHERN LIGHTS CAUSED BY GAY MARRIAGE

The Northern Lights are a sign that God approves of gay marriage, according to pro-European Christians.

80% of men are twats

THE majority of men are either meatheads or vain self-absorbed idiots, it has emerged.

Researchers at the Institute for Studies found over three-quarters of adult males were very hard to like.

Professor Henry Brubaker said: "Socialising with young men, we found that they either wanted to show off about their material possessions, punch you in the face for no reason, or some senseless combination of the two.

"It's maybe not their fault, rather they are the hapless victims of a culture that teaches them to value steroids, toiletries and morally vacuous sales jobs rather than channeling their unblinkered self-belief into something vaguely worthwhile."

Tom Logan, 23, said: "I'm torn between instinctive interests in art and nature, and a mainstream culture that tells me to get rich, love nothing and 'nail loads of fanny'.

"I think I'm going to keep buying loads of pec-revealing designer t-shirts until the point of me becomes clear."

A EUROPHILE Christian councillor from Oxfordshire has claimed that Britain is basking in God's love and the aurora borealis is a 'massive heavenly thumbs up' to same sex unions.

Councillor Stephen Malley said: "I predicted this would happen if parliament passed the gay marriage bill and I am delighted to have been proved right.

"God is love and every once in a while he hammers home the point by filling the sky with a multitude of beautiful colours.

"I wish he would do it more often but, let's be honest, people are shits."

A spokesman for the Pro-European Christians said the organisation embraced Councillor Malley's remarks and said it was a '100% ac-

curate reflection of their beliefs'.

Councillor Malley caused controversy last year after demanding a massive increase in the aid budget and referring to Britain as 'Morris-Dancey Land'.

He also described women who did not clean behind the fridge as 'Jesus-like' and gave Channel Four News reporter Michael Crick a five-minute cuddle.

Scotland not allowed to use British oxygen

A deafening klaxon will sound every time some oxygen passes over this wall

British oxygen molecules that drift into Scotland must be sent back immediately, it has been claimed.

THE leaders of the three main political parties warned that Scotland has no automatic right to use Britain's sovereign gases.

Prime minister, David Cameron, said: "If the Scottish Nationalists think there is going to be a free-flow of gases back and forth across the border then it's obvious they know very little about the nature of gas. Gases like to stay put. In much the same way as water."

Nick Clegg, the self-styled 'deputy prime minister', said: "I would prefer to breathe Franco-German oxygen. I also think that Scottish people should breathe Franco-German oxygen, I just don't think they should be allowed to breathe British oxygen if they're not British anymore.

"So, anyway, that's what I think."

Meanwhile, Labour's Ed Miliband warned:

"We'll know if you've breathed our oxygen because, when we get it back, it won't be oxygen anymore. It'll be carbon dioxide.

"I used to be the energy minister, so I'm basically a scientist."

Bill McKay, from Edinburgh, said: "Oh well, that's that. You can't just 'make' oxygen. Or maybe you can.

"I've really no idea."

Scotland joining Eurovision would be 'very difficult for everyone'

SCOTLAND'S bid to join Eurovision would be opposed by countries where people can hear, it has been claimed.

Manuel Barroso, the president of Eurovision, said: "The other members will not stand by while Scotland unleashes some kind of auto-tuned bagpipe shitfest.

"It would, no doubt, be performed by an ageing, kilted, soft-core punk. I'm seeing horrible visions of a 'Scottish Tenpole Tudor'.

"Either that or they'll offer up Hue and Cry and expect us all to just sit there and take it."

But Scotland's first minister, Alex Salmond, dismissed Mr Barroso, insisting he already has a detailed Eurovision plan, entitled *The Coercion of Primal Scream*.

Some rich prick racks up five-figure bar bill in pathetic attempt at popularity

Wealthy idiot Tom Logan has spent over £54,000 in a dreadful bar, in a vain effort to make others like him.

LOGAN, who probably does something involving finance, undertook his sad and grotesque display of wealth in a cold and soulless City bar called D-Luxe.

Onlooker Roy Hobbs said: "He was ordering these bottles of champagne with sparklers in.

"They were brought to the table by sexy girls with fixed grins and empty eyes.

"Everyone gathered around his booth, not because they liked him but because he was giving away free drinks.

"The whole dynamic of the situation was almost unbearably pathetic and an affront to all that is decent.

"Then they brought out this massive bottle that was the length of a car, it took six people to carry it.

"Everyone was cheering and the DJ put on some special music. But it was all a pretence, the atmosphere was hollow and everyone in the room was somehow cheapened just by being there."

Hobbs added: "I don't remember what he looked like.

"Probably he was big and slightly paunchy with a black open-necked shirt, fluffy slicked-back hair and deck shoes. Could be wrong though.

"Don't suppose it matters anyway."

And then they all went home

Good-looking groups of friends unable to sustain conversation

GROUPS of people who socialise together because they are all attractive run out of conversation very quickly, it has emerged.

Researchers found that 'hot' people with 'hot' friends engage in shared activities such as standing next to each other, taking group photos and saying 'hello' and 'goodbye'.

Professor Henry Brubaker, of the Institute for Studies, said: "They do have brief conversations about body hair removal, but mostly they just stare into space."

He added: "Some good-looking friendship groups often include a token 'funny one' who is fat.

"This can extend conversations for up to three minutes, but the less attractive one is essentially a decoy designed to show the group has depth of character.

"Never forget, all good-looking people are evil."

fuckr

The new social network connecting people who just want to swear abusively

Everything the internet is for, condensed into one handy app:
- ● Insult your friends and family anonymously!
- ● Troll celebrities anywhere, any time!
- ● Special feature making Wikipedia vandalism even easier!
- ● Also streams porn, obviously!

The Daily Mash Guide to ...
Romania and Bulgaria

They will soon be flooding over here for botched operations, meagre benefits and racist taunting.

But how much do we really know about the Romanians and the Bulgish?

- Romanian immigrant **Dracula**, who sneaked into the country via lax border controls on Whitby shipwrecks, came to violate our women and undercut hard-working local plumbers.

- **Great Uncle Bulgaria**, ambassador to Britain since the late 1970s, ran a gang of scavenging lowlives illegally occupying public land. He was arrested by Operation Yew Tree earlier this year.

- Britain fought for years to release both countries from the iron grip of **Communism**. But experts stress that being freed from Communism does not mean freedom of movement and access to free markets.

- Like all Europeans, Eastern Europeans have a history of **anti-Semitism**. This means it is perfectly okay to spread lies about them.

- Thousands of British people have bought cheap holiday apartments in **Bulgarian ski resorts**. Studies have shown that cleaning these apartments should provide enough employment for everyone in Bulgaria.

- Romanians are rumoured to **drink heavily**, treat women like chattel and engage in bare-knuckle brawls. Experts say that to the average Romanian, most British towns will seem like a fancy tea party.

Middle class 'just working class people with nicer stuff'

Middle class people share 100% of their genetic material with working class people, it has emerged.

RESEARCHERS at the Institute for Studies found that the differences between the two classes were entirely cultural.

Professor Henry Brubaker said: "Falling living standards among the middle class have prompted an identity crisis, with many professionals desperately hoping their DNA would continue to set them apart after the Waitrose budget dries up.

"However, while the upper class is extra-terrestrial in origin there is no biological distinction between the two lower tiers of our society.

"You may think you've come a long way, but you're probably just one brioche away from being a prole."

Mother-of-two Emma Bradford said: "Our only hope is to keep buying stuff.

"We could only afford two middle class things this week, a pomegranate to put in salad and one of those round cheeses that you bake in the oven.

"In the evenings we gather around the cheese and look at it, as if a message of hope might manifest on its rubbery exterior."

Only the dog is not of common stock

"Yep, it's a dog - £100 please"

VETS TAKING THE ABSOLUTE PISS

VETS are charging up to £70 to stick a needle in a cat, it has emerged.

Researchers found that despite not even being qualified to look after people, veterinary surgeons are charging large sums to perform animal operations that are revolting but probably not very hard.

Professor Henry Brubaker of the Institute for Studies said: "Britons love their pets more than any human family members, so animal doctors charge a fucking fortune to keep them alive.

"They have absolutely no qualms about selling you special cat food, vitamin-enhanced goldfish water and expensive insurance that covers your dog for space travel.

"Then after making a big song and dance about your pet's health, they're quite happy to kill it for you when it gets a bit knackered."

Vet Tom Booker said: "You have to study for five years, although a lot of that is playing rugby and having sex with agricultural crudents.

"You wouldn't believe the creatures some people want me to heal. Someone brought in a rat the other day. A rat!

"Still, we got a couple of hundred quid for selling them some rat ointment."

Irish name pronounced how it's written

Kyla Burns has surprised her colleagues by revealing there are no hidden letters in her name.

Staff at London accountants Madeley-Finnegan greeted her warmly, but became visibly nervous when the time came to add her name to the tea and coffee rota.

Colleague Nathan Muir said: "She seemed nice, but we got burned last month when Aisling Kelley visited from the Dublin office.

"I'm not accusing every Irish person of smuggling a few extra letters in their name, but that's exactly how they get away with it.

"So you can imagine our relief when Kyla spelled her name and every single letter could be accounted for – like a proper name."

Meanwhile, a name badge reading 'Kaieyloagh Ní Byrnes' was thrown in the bin moments before Kyla was taken on a tour of the office.

Irish names have been a constant source of irritation to the English since the 19th century, when many Irish families started hoarding extra letters in case of a shortage.

Man with Royal Mail shares thinks he's Gordon Gekko

OFFICE worker Tom Booker reckons he is real hot shit after potentially making £350 on Royal Mail shares.

Booker, who now closely identifies himself with Michael Douglas's *Wall Street* character Gordon Gekko, said: "I scented blood and I went for the kill. To the victor the spoils."

First-time investor Booker arrived at work today sporting a pair of red braces purchased from Tie Rack.

He was later overheard by colleagues wondering how many 'hookers' and how much cocaine he could get with a sum in the region of £350.

Booker said: "Fuck all you chumps and losers. Now if you'll excuse me, time is money. And money is power."

The real Gordon Gekko

Public 'nowhere near ready' for reversible USB

It just does

People are today trying to comprehend the 'reversible' version of an object known to most as 'thing'.

EXPERTS stressed that as none of you understand why the existing USB connection works, making it 'reversible' will lead to unnecessary staring.

IT consultant Nathan Muir said: "We should just have started making them without telling anybody. No-one would have noticed and there would be no questions."

Martin Bishop, a computer user from Stevenage, said: "I use the thing to put stuff into the computer, so when I 'reverse' it will it take stuff out of the computer?

"And if it does, do I have to make sure that all the little bits of digital electricity are facing the right way before I put them back in?"

Jane Thompson, from Peterborough, said: "What about my photographs? Will they still be photographs? Or will they be the opposite of photographs?"

Muir stressed that the reversible USB would 'neuter the advantage of Apple's lightning cable' before realising what he had said.

Bishop added: "What, in the name of God, is a 'lightning cable'?"

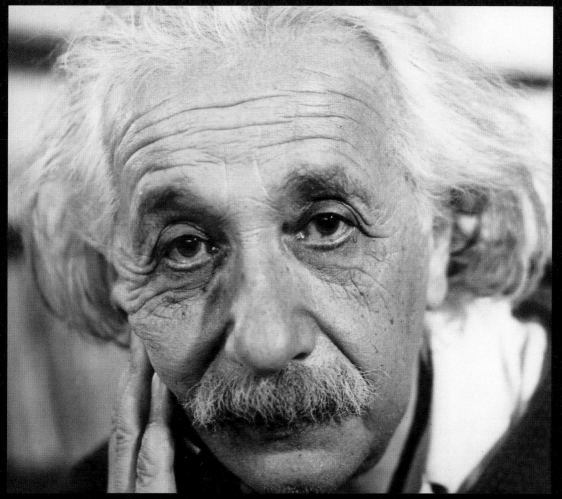

Had visible wrinkles and eye bags

People who do worthwhile things have shit clothes and hair

Individuals who achieve useful things do not care about looking or smelling good, it has been confirmed.

THE Institute for Studies found that contrary to widely-held beliefs there is no link between physical attractiveness and being worthy of respect.

Professor Henry Brubaker said: "People who get off their arses to make and discover things tend not to look like celebrities. In fact they

quite often have clothing that smells like it's been left in the washing machine for too long.

"This is because useful people have more pressing things on their minds than having awesome trousers, abs or a memorable silhouette.

"For example, Einstein's hair looked like that because that's how

it came out of his head, sometimes he hacked at it with scissors but only when it got in his eyes.

"It wasn't a self-conscious attempt at a 'mad professor vibe'."

Prof Brubaker added: "You can be entirely obsessed with your self-image, but you will end up working in a fashionable bar until you die."

Hull pledges a 'shitload' of culture

THE city of Hull last night pledged to show Britain what culture really is, especially if you are into magicians.

After being named UK City of Culture 2017, Hull insisted it would put on a year of events that would be 'very classy, even the ones with an intense focus on gratuitous nudity'.

John Prescott, the city's former MP, said: "We are going to culture the fuck out of this."

A council spokesman added: "People in Hull like magicians. When Paul Daniels was here a couple of years ago he needed a police escort. It was mental.

"Beyond that we'll probably have some fancy dancing and a guy who can eat a bike."

Prescott has offered to do a painting of a big pie

PARALLELS WITH FIRST WORLD WAR DOING HISTORIAN'S HEAD IN

The parallels with the First World War are totally doing a historian's head in, it has been confirmed.

JULIAN Cook, professor of early 20th Century history at Roehampton University, has admitted he dreads reading the newspapers because 'it is just one massive headfuck after another'.

He said: "It's got to the stage where my wife won't let me speak. All I'm allowed to do is point at the front page of the *Guardian* while looking at her with an expression of sheer horror.

"We have a strongly nationalistic, strategically significant eastern European country deciding its fate, while three empires stand waiting in the wings, rattling their sabres. It is freaking me the fuck out."

He added: "I talk to my historian pals and they're like, 'no way, that's totally what I was thinking'. And then we all shout 'powder keg' in unison and have a bit of a giggle.

"It relieves the tension, but seriously, we're all terrified."

Professor Cook said the fact it was also the 100th anniversary of the First World War was 'spooky'.

"Honestly, you want to try being a historian at the moment. Mental."

Difference between old and new Xbox not obvious to women

WOMEN last night admitted they had failed to spot the massive leap forward in gaming between the Xbox 360 and the Xbox One.

Experts said the £430 device is a game-changing console that more than justifies an absolutely tremendous amount of fuss.

But Joanna Kramer, from Exeter, said: "Haven't you already got this game? With the cars racing around? Haven't you had it for ages?

"Oh I see, that was Forza 4 and this one's Forza 5. But is it still just driving cars around, or can you do different stuff now?"

Kramer's boyfriend Tom Logan, said: "Can't you see the light bloom, the added draw distance, the anti-aliasing? And what a frame rate.

"God, just look at the detail in those textures."

ENGLAND WINS THE WORLD CUP

page 80

Gary Barlow & Simon Cowell believe in themselves

pages 67 and 86

thedailymash

www.thedailymash.co.uk

RANDOM ACTS OF FOUL-MOUTHED CRUELTY

Monday 2015

Hundreds of lost indie bands found in Camden Lock

More than 300 indie bands have been discovered in Camden Lock after it was drained for repairs

THE musicians, caked in thick mud and entangled with shopping trolleys, empty cider cans and discarded crack cocaine wrappers, are being cleaned and restored by volunteers.

One particularly tough knot of human detritus turned out to be Shed Seven, The Shop Assistants and Klaxons.

Workman Tom Logan said: "Once the worst of the filth was cleaned off, they got Shed Seven running and we heard a brief burst of *Going For Gold* before they stuttered to a halt."

The bands, thought to have blundered into the canal while drunk and wearing shades at night, are being pieced together by volunteers who have appealed for help from anyone who read the NME between the late 80s and 2002.

EMI executive Joseph Turner said: "It's all very well putting these bands back together, but there's only a limited amount of mid-afternoon festival slots and I want those kept free for younger, more attractive folktronica acts."

Conservationist Carolyn Ryan described the find as "a living relic of more androgynous times".

She said: "Working out whether a man in skinny jeans was a member of the Wombats, the Guillemots or the Pigeon Detectives is very hard.

"And drummers often have no idea what band they were in because they were at the back and not paying attention."

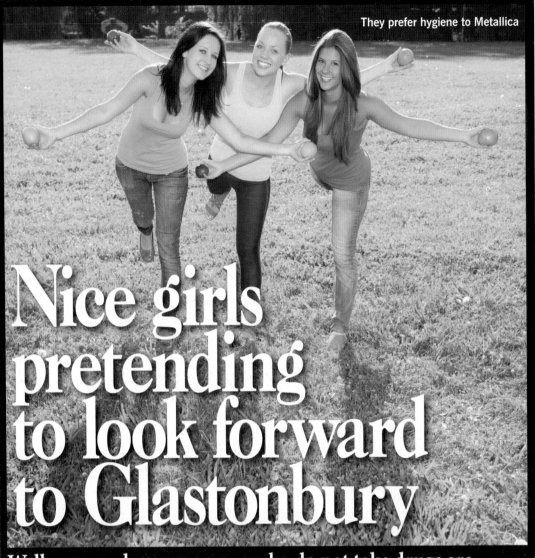

They prefer hygiene to Metallica

Nice girls pretending to look forward to Glastonbury

Well-groomed young women who do not take drugs are pretending to be excited about attending Glastonbury Festival.

THE conventional, upbeat women are focusing on the practicalities of the weekend, like whether to bring an inflatable pillow, to avoid considering the hellish reality of survival in a massive ditch.

Sixth-former Nikki Hollis said: "Apart from living like an animal and hating all the acts, this is going to be the best weekend of my life.

"It's great that my boyfriend Tom is insisting we see Metallica, who he's suddenly got into, because seeing them live will prob-

ably overcome my previous intense dislike of thrash metal.

"Obviously everyone else will be talking disjointed drug shit while I sit and watch, but I don't mind. I'll just think about my nice clean duvet and food that hasn't been made by dirty hippies in a van."

However, others are struggling to maintain their enthusiasm for seeing Dolly Parton in an ironic way while simultaneously faced with chemical toilets full of

hundreds of clearly visible turds.

Durham University student Joanna Kramer said: "My friend Charlotte said she wouldn't mind not washing her hair for a few days, which was clearly a lie because she owns a bottle of conditioner that cost £95.

"I wanted to tell her that none of us wanted to go to Glastonbury, but then it would have looked as though I didn't want to go to Glastonbury. It's a conspiracy of silence."

"I adjust well to warm climates and foreign food"

Blair applies to be Caliph

FORMER prime minister Tony Blair has submitted his CV to the newly-declared Islamic Caliphate in the Middle East.

Already hugely successful in his role as Middle East peace envoy, Blair believes he is perfectly suited to be the unquestioned supreme leader of a new Islamist era.

He said: "I was instrumental in creating networks of Islamic extremists in Iraq and Afghanistan using an innovative mix of aerial bombings and ground invasions.

"There are very few jihadis who wouldn't name Tony Blair and Operation Iraqi Liberation as their direct inspiration.

"And I am already a figure both universally known and universally hated in the West, which is great positioning for ISIS."

A spokesman for ISIS agreed that Blair's credentials were impressive, but had doubts about his commitment and thought the tie he wore for the interview was too colourful.

Dubai unveils Twatopolis

A MASSIVE dome full of the horrible things that twats like is to be built in Dubai.

The quintrillion-dollar air-conditioned monstrosity will contain ghastly hotels, pretentious shops and soulless bars called things like 'Tyger'.

A government spokesman said:

"Twatopolis will consolidate our city's status as a hub for the biggest twats on the planet.

"Footballers, their dreadful wives, sleazebag billionaires and cackling middle-management hen parties will come in their droves because it is very big, very expensive and the weather is hot."

Footballer Wayne Hayes said: "Can I buy shoes that cost more than a hospital? Are they very colourful and can I carry them away in big shiny bags? Can I then eat a burger while my wife gets some hot 'healing mud' poured on her? And then buy some shit art?

"Is it vile? If so, I'm in."

FEATURE

The Daily Mash Guide to ...
Public Speaking

Delivering a speech or presentation is many humans' greatest fear.

Here's how to successfully address a room:

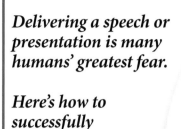

- Build rapport by telling the audience something personal about yourself, for example how you killed a man in Belgium and hid his body in a lorry depot.

- Correct body language suggests status and confidence. Lie in the centre of the stage and curl into the fetal position. Then you can command the room, like a commanding foetus.

- Imagine your audience naked. Better still, imagine them naked and living in a network of underground caverns ruled over by merciless robot overlords called mandroids.

- Carry a matchbox pet in your breast pocket, for example a grasshopper. It'll give you a sense of companionship, also you can talk to it, building anticipation by asking the box questions like "Do you think they're ready for the first quarter sales figures, Mr Feelers?"

- Take regular sips from a glass of your own urine, which is known to cleanse the liver.

- Warm up the crowd with some light bullying of audience members with distinguishing physical features. Also if you forget bits of your speech you can simply turn to your victim and ask 'You still here, wonky eye man?' in a snidey voice.

- If it's going badly, use up your time allowance by individually offering everyone in the room a Malteser.

Your problems solved, with *Holly Harper*

Granny's ox-tongue surprise wasn't a massive hit

People just want to worship their false consumer gods

Dear Holly,

The wife has put me on a stupid vegan diet until Christmas. I'm pretending it's ok but I fear I won't make it much longer without taking a bite from one of her magnificent succulent thighs. Help!

Jay-Z
Los Angeles

Dear Holly,

Having just watched the new John Lewis Christmas advert I have realised people don't need me anymore: they just want to worship their false consumer gods and edit out the last shred of traditional Christmas spirit to make way for cute woodland creatures accompanied by Lily Allen singing a Keane song. Satan truly has vanquished the Earth. So I'm considering a career change: Mayor of Toronto or head of the Cooperative Bank seem to come with good perks. What do you think?

Santa
Lapland

Dear Jay-Z,

There's a girl in my class called Francesca Solomon who is a strict vegan. She's not allowed to eat any nice things, including Haribo Star Mix, which no doubt makes for a pretty miserable existence. To cheer her up I once invited her round to my granny's house for tea, which was probably a bad idea because the only food my granny eats comes from animals that have spent their lives in total darkness and then been mercilessly slaughtered. Although granny's ox-tongue surprise wasn't a massive hit with Francesca, at least the evening ended on a high when granny's dog Bilko thanked Francesca on behalf of the animal kingdom by forcefully humping her school bag. Hope that helps!

Holly xx

Dear Santa,

You should probably see your school careers officer so you know what direction to take. And don't worry, these days, the system's not all geared towards academia. When you first arrive you'll be given a short interview, asked to complete an aptitude test and then your future career will be revealed. For a dramatic edge, our careers officer likes to set 'the reveal' to climactic pop music! anything by Snow Patrol or Adele and you'll be trotting off to study sports science at Loughborough University, but if you hear the intro to I'll Stand By You by the Pretenders then you're looking at a part-time job in Costa for the forseeable future.

Hope that helps!
Holly xx

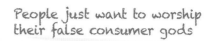

Your astrological week ahead, with **Psychic Bob**

Aries
21 Mar-19 Apr
Thursday, 6.15pm. I can't say what, exactly, but that's when it'll happen.

Taurus
20 Apr – 20 May
You wake up and smell the coffee. You live alone. WHO IS MAKING COFFEE IN YOUR KITCHEN?

Gemini
21 May-20 Jun
This week you play the film *Gandhi* backwards and watch a zombie rise from the grave to enslave the whole of India.

Cancer
21 Jun-22 Jul
On Saturday you will take a satisfying final gulp from your beer, only to see there's another unsatisfyingly small gulp left in the bottom.

Leo
23 Jul-22 Aug
You're justifiably proud of 'never shitting on your own doorstep' but what about the other 43 entirely undeserving householders?

Virgo
23 Aug-22 Sep
With the death of Pete Seeger, you feel it's an apt time to find out who on earth he was.

Libra
23 Sep-23 Oct
Thanks to Buzzfeed you can now only read stuff if it's written in list form. You're currently enjoying James Joyce's '14,298 Facts About Leo Bloom'.

Scorpio
24 Oct-21 Nov
All razors are disposable razors, if you think about it.

Sagittarius
22 Nov-21 Dec
Uh-oh. The reincarnation of Homer has turned up to question your use of the word 'epic' about a night out in Wetherspoons. This is awkward.

Capricorn
22 Dec-19 Jan
Your new-found focus at work leads to you screaming 'Take it, BITCH' as you feed paper into the document shredder.

Aquarius
20 Jan-19 Feb
Remember, never say something in print that you wouldn't say to that person's face, you big sack of piss.

Pisces
20 Feb-20 Mar
Nobody gives a shit about your opinion on Woody Allen. Nobody.

This one's about having too much spare time

Retired people flooding UK with shit art

Britain's retired people are producing overwhelming amounts of poor quality artwork, experts have warned.

ART industry insiders have warned that unless people in their 60s can be dissuaded from churning out paintings of dogs and landscapes the market will implode.

Gallerist Tom Logan said: "With an ageing population, the UK has more and more retired people exploring the artistic potential they mistakenly think they possess.

"Typically these pictures are titled Bicycles, Family, or Peaceful Beach. Often they are sold at small galleries that are also bistros.

"Exhibitions of retired art are lucrative because relatives feel emotionally blackmailed into buying pictures of themselves, even if the strange proportions make them look like the big guy from *The Goonies*.

"No-one wants to buy good art any more because their houses are already full of pictures by their parents and grandparents."

66-year-old Mary Fisher said: "I started painting as a hobby but my friends say my vivid use of colours on works like Rainbow and Tree are really eye-catching. Maybe I am the next Picasso."

Retired civil servant Stephen Malley said: "I've even done a modern art piece, Blocks, and made some ceramic hedgehogs.

"After I've conquered the art world I might write an espionage thriller called something like The Dragon Process.

"Then I will die."

Most people don't understand the things they say

THE majority of people just repeat popular words and phrases without knowing what they mean.

The Institute for Studies found that most human interaction was simply repetition of clichéd phrases and ideas learned from TV, the internet and people who are considered clever.

Humans generally have no idea of the meanings of the words they are saying, but are simply mimicking sounds.

Professor Henry Brubaker said: "We found that most communication consisted of well-worn phrases such as 'You could not make it up', 'It's a no-brainer' and 'Coffee through nose moment!'

"Other popular utterances included 'England could do with another goal', 'Duck is quite a fatty meat' and 'Clegg is a shithead'.

"Humans are clearly not the creative, highly evolved mammals we imagined, and I now believe we are more similar genetically to parrots or photocopiers."

Professor Brubaker added that an aversion to original thought could explain a number of mysteries that have baffled scientists, such as the popularity of the *Fast and Furious* films and the newspaper columns of Allison Pearson.

Marketing manager Donna Sheridan said: "The idea that we all just repeat things we've heard sounds like rubbish to me. These scientists should come down from their ivory towers and try living in the real world.

"I have original thoughts all the time, but that's probably because I'm a Pisces and pisceans are very creative."

Hen parties embark on lifeless parody of fun

Thousands of hen parties are preparing for raucous yet entirely fake fun.

AS the hen party season begins, groups of women are booking hotel rooms in Bath where they will pretend to enjoy doing outrageous but strangely dull things.

Emma Bradford, a 31 year-old bride-to-be, said: "We had something called a 'pamper day' then we put on special t-shirts, each printed with a single word that summarises our personality.

"Mine said 'cocklover' which was a bit awkward as my nan was with us.

"Then I was given a list of tasks, like kissing a bald man's head, something involving a dildo, etcetera etcetera.

"Everyone was laughing a lot, but in a quite forced way because the whole experience felt really empty, although nobody acknowledged that."

Bradford's sister-in-law Nikki Hollis said: "I remember dancing in a big group to 80s music.

My arms felt really tired and I just wanted to be in bed.

"There was a married estate agent who kept poking me in the back with his erection.

"One of Emma's work friends said a racist thing to a shopkeeper, I lost my mobile and Donna 'the mental one' turned out to have legitimate mental health problems.

"The evening ended abruptly when we all had a massive argument about nothing."

South East finally being wiped clean by the wrath of God

SAHARAN sand is sweeping across Britain's greediest and most materialistic region, erasing its temples of avarice and sending a stark warning to all those who would worship at the altar of Mammon.

Dr Marcus Brody, an expert in Biblical weather, said: "Like the sandstorm that consumed Tanis, it will probably last a whole year and will destroy much of London as well as Colchester, Basildon and, of course, Peterborough, the final resting place of the Ark of the Covenant.

"By caring for nothing but money and objects, the south east – and its pharaoh, Boris Johnson – have tested the patience of the Great Yahweh, or 'Jehovah'.

"Now He is cleansing them with an abrasive substance that will reach into every corner of their souls leaving them as hollow, crumbling shells, staring forever at their greed and folly.

"So you should probably stay indoors today."

FEATURE

Gary Barlow: I really believe… I can make everyone hate me again

IT'S been a long road for me, from the first Take That days through my wilderness years to being back with the boys on top of the world.

But I've kept myself together through it all because I truly believe, in my heart, that I can make everyone in the country hate me again.

Remember in the 1990s, when Gary Barlow was a universally derided joke? When I got dropped by my record company and ballooned to 34 stone in weight, a bitter, lonely recluse?

Those were the days. And, with the release of a new solo album and that advert with the meerkats, I think they're on their way back.

It may sound egotistical, but I can feel the festering resentment out there from everyone who fell for the new humble, slimmed down me back in 2006.

And every time I destroy a dream on the X-Factor, using the platform given to me to stamp on a young hopeful's fingers, it's a little closer to breaking through.

It's taken a lot of work. Organising that Diamond Jubilee concert sowed the first seeds of unease, and coming out as a grasping, tax-dodging Tory really turned opinion-formers against me.

But it's next year, when I release a new Take That album where I don't allow the other boys to sing and kick Robbie Williams out of the band live on stage, that'll really do it.

I can't wait to stand in the middle of that stadium, tens of thousands of women booing as they realise what an utter prick I've been all along. I'll be there, arms outstretched, basking in their hatred.

And then I'll start on the pies.

SINKHOLES ARE BADGERS' REVENGE

Sinkholes appearing across Britain are an act of revenge by the badgers.

THE badgers claimed responsibility for the holes which have swallowed houses, vehicles and at least 20 cows.

In a statement, the badgers said the holes were a 'legitimate response' to the government's 'acts of war' and threatened to 'hollow out Britain until it was like an Easter egg'.

The statement added: "You think we are beneath you. Well, we are beneath you. Literally. What about that, eh?

"Admit to your TB lies and pay us reparations or one day the ground you stand on will suddenly give way and you will be plunged into darkness.

"And in that darkness will be a righteous badger, waiting to bite your face off."

The government stressed it was trying not to be intimidated by the badgers, but urged everyone to put their ears to their living room floors and listen for scratching, digging and swearing.

A spokesman said: "If you hear the badgers you must phone the army and then get into your car and drive as fast as you can in any direction for at least 24 hours."

Prime minister David Cameron added: "This is very frightening. I am terrified."

Tesco vows to take Britain down with it

TESCO has warned the people of the UK that they will pay with their lives for abandoning it.

The supermarket, which has seen profits fall for the second year in a row, is determined to go out in a blaze of glory rather than fade away like Fine Fare.

The operation will begin with riots at Tesco stores caused by rock-bottom prices and the offer of 10,000 Clubcard points for the head of a rival supermarket employee.

Once in control of the nation's food supplies, Tesco will draft young men for a bloody civil war

against the government fighting from Tesco Extra strongholds.

Tesco Metros will become munitions dumps for urban warfare, with a Tesco Local in every neighbourhood housing enough stackers-turned-soldiers to enforce a curfew.

Mary Fisher of Crawley said: "I shop at Tesco, I bank with Tesco, my mobile phone is with Tesco, and they've made it clear they know all my secrets.

"But when has the government ever given me a third off pork loin steaks?"

Of course I smoke crack, says Boris

Boris Johnson has admitted being 'on the pipe'.

FOLLOWING the moving confession by Toronto's mayor that he had dabbled in crack, Boris Johnson admitted that he too was partial to the invigorating substance.

He said: "Obviously I smoke crack, or 'the mayor's friend' as I prefer to call it.

"London life is all about highs and lows – the incredible euphoria of shopping on Bond Street, the crushing despair of living in a Wood Green bedsit.

"I tried understanding the city by reading lots of Peter Ackroyd books, but they didn't really give me those extreme emotions like crack does.

"Also it gives me great ideas, like my plan to build an airport in the middle of a river."

87% of Londoners had already worked it out

Political analyst Julian Cook said: "Illegal drugs make up 40 per cent of London's economy and 100 per cent of its recreational activity, so it's logical that we have a mayor who is an out-and-proud basehead."

Londoner Joanna Kramer said: "That's why I voted for Boris, because he's sweaty and unkempt which in my impressionable mind equates to personality.

"I don't mind if he smokes crack, he earns a good salary so he should be able to keep it together."

Boris Johnson added: "I'm not ashamed to be a man of the people. You think I live in a big fancy house in West London, actually it's a squat with all the copper stripped out and pigeons nesting in the bathroom."

Peter Hitchens urged to try teensy bit of meth

PETER Hitchens, the anti-drugs journalist, has been urged to try the teensiest bit of methamphetamine to prove his theory that addiction does not exist.

Professor Henry Brubaker, of the Institute for Studies, said: "I would start him off with just a soupçon. Most people find that's enough to completely ruin their lives.

"At that point, if he is correct, he will simply choose not to turn his life into a raging sea of shit."

"It's as if he doesn't have any willpower."

Professor Brubaker added:

"Like climate sceptics, Peter's politics degree makes him an expert at all kinds of science.

"I was having lunch with him once and he started coughing terribly. I told him to get it checked out and he nodded and then phoned James Delingpole from the Telegraph. They both agreed that Peter's cough was a Marxist conspiracy.

"I told him he should really see a doctor but he said that James has a degree in English literature and was therefore more than qualified to diagnose left-wing pulmonary infections."

Sometimes the maverick voices turn out to be right. But mostly they don't.

I only want Scotland to be independent so I can destroy it, admits Salmond

Alex Salmond has finally admitted he hates Scotland and wants the country to be independent so he can abolish it.

THE Scottish first minister insisted his fellow countrymen are the worst people in the world who spend most of their time 'either threatening to kill you, or vomiting on you'.

He said: "I can't keep lying. It's a hellhole filled with drunken nutters, ghastly housing estates and food that is simply disgusting.

"I'm going to win independence, bankrupt the place, set fire to the buildings and then move to France – as long as there aren't any Scottish people there.

"I want to leave this place a wasteland, populated only by scavenging piss-artists and thousands of bastard folk singers.

"Now I've finally come clean, I suspect I will have the backing of the vast majority of Scots, who all hate each other as much as I hate every single one of them."

Mr Salmond also revealed he 'loves the way Vladimir Putin holds ordinary Russians in utter contempt' and would gladly hand Scotland's economy to the terrifying president and his gangster cronies.

He added: "All Scottish people are sexual deviants."

"Hell. Hole."

Miliband denies your right to make massively ill-informed decision

ED Miliband is to deny you the right to make a cretinous, ill-informed choice about Europe.

Writing in the *Financial Times*, the Labour leader said there was 'no way you are getting anywhere near this' if he has anything to do with it.

He added: "I have travelled all over Britain talking to people about the EU and it is perfectly clear that you don't know the first fucking thing about it.

"Most of you seem to think it's about Abu Hamza and cucumbers.

"I was talking to this particularly dense woman in Peterborough and she just kept going on and on about cucumbers. Eventually I screamed, 'shut up!' right in her face. And then she chased me into a park.

"So, anyway. Too important. You're all idiots. Forget it."

The Labour leader also said that he was going to take more of your money 'because you spend it like a child'.

Wood burning stove brings authenticity to middle class man's life

The purchase of a wood burning stove means that a middle class man's life is no longer superficial.

36-YEAR-OLD web designer Stephen Malley found that he is much more real and grounded since buying a stove that wood goes into.

He said: "I've got a heap of logs. Logs made from trees. Actual trees, from forests.

"I handle the logs."

Malley had been concerned that his desk-based job, consumerist lifestyle and inability to stop thinking about money had left him somehow removed from the natural world.

He said: "Now that I'm burning wood on a regular basis, I feel that I've returned to a primal state. A sort of rugged innocence, if you will.

"I am basically a caveman, except my cave is a house that has an Apple product in every room and several large books of contemporary art prints.

"Next thing is to buy an axe, although I need to call the council first to find out if I need an axe licence."

Rugged, solid, earthy etc

Middle class families standing round unsolicited tabloid newspaper on doormat

MIDDLE class families have gathered around a tabloid newspaper that was put through their letter box without permission.

The families are staring at their free copy of the *Sun*, unsure what to do with it.

Martin Bishop, from Hatfield, told his wife and children: "Don't touch it, I'm going to try and open it using this umbrella. Nice and easy, there we go. Now then…

"Lots of capital letters. Lots of words in bold. Big photographs. Short articles. And my goodness, what a lot of puns. Okay, right.

"Well, it's not very nice but I don't think it's anything to be worried about. It's just a newspaper for people who do not prioritise education in quite the same way as we do."

Bishop added: "Emily, could you be a poppet, nip out to the garage and get my barbecue tongs and one of the green, heavy-duty binbags?"

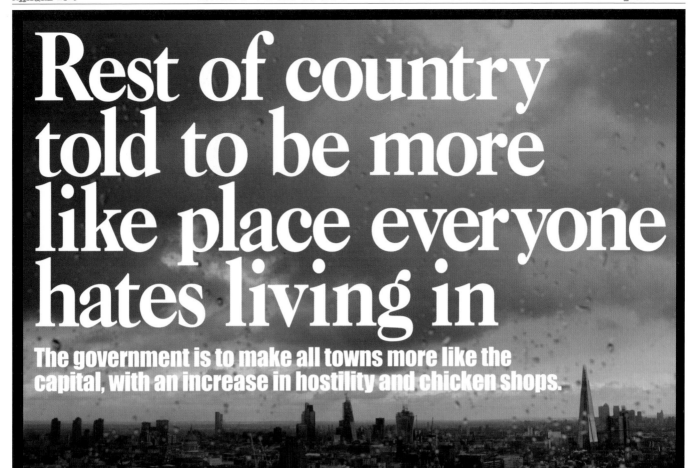

Rest of country told to be more like place everyone hates living in

The government is to make all towns more like the capital, with an increase in hostility and chicken shops.

Yes to buildings that look like cocks

IN order to ensure full Londonification is in place by 2015, business secretary Vince Cable has announced that everyone's rent or mortgage payments will be doubled with immediate effect.

Properties that become unaffordable will be seized and donated to sandwich shop chain Pret A Manger.

Cable said: "London is one of the most expensive cities in the world, but has an unrivalled reputation when it comes to galleries, theatre and public toilets in railway stations.

"If we make houses equally, cripplingly expensive across the country, we think every town could get its own Tate. Maybe even a Jamie's Italian too."

London blogger Wayne Hayes, whose website My City's Shitter Than Your City attracts over a million hits a month, said: "My livelihood is based on pointing out the whimsical, specific aspects of London life, like riding on the bus and eating bagels.

"I refuse to share my spotlight with people from the provinces."

Helen Archer, a teacher living in Somerset said: "A few of my school friends moved to London and they're always boasting about how their rents got so high that they had to move to Zone 5.

"I can't wait to find out what that actually means."

Prince George begins boarding school

THE five-month-old heir to the British throne has started his first term at Gordonstoun preparatory school.

The public school will be the young Prince's home for the next decade and will haunt him until the end of his days.

Gordonstoun will teach the young Prince walking and other basic motor skills. From this foundation he will learn to play cricket and rugby while being shielded from the very existence of football.

Royal historian Denys Finch-Hatton said: "The regime of freezing cold showers, grouse genocide and fagging for louche, predatory three-year-olds will soon demolish any hint of empathy for other human beings."

The Daily Mash Guide to ...
Surviving a Heatwave

THE sun is out and everyone is going to perish – except you.

With the heatwave predicted to continue throughout July, the average human's chances of survival are virtually nil. Here's how to improve your odds:

- Build a machine like a tank but with a massive drill on the end. Then tunnel down through the Earth's crust, reaching a more temperate land where prehistoric tribes live alongside giant dinosaur-like lizards. Rescue a beautiful cave girl who is cornered by a rival tribe. Her name will be something like Ti-Wa. Then run off into the jungle to eat strange fruit and have sex.

- Desk work can be hell in the heat so get some time off by staring at the sun until you go blind. Then you can legitimately say you can't see your computer screen, because your retinas have been incinerated.

- Extreme heat will make you sweaty, but beware that some deodorants can cause you to be pursued by a horde of very attractive young women, literally falling over each other to have sex with you. Be sure to ask for a deodorant that doesn't make you too sexually magnetic.

- Scientists say that drinking alcohol in the sun seriously increases your risk of dehydration. But then scientists say all sorts of things.

- If you're feeling sorry for yourself, spare a thought for the millions of people who live on the sun. The Sunnians have to deal with extreme temperatures literally every day.

- Get an electric fan. These are also great for giving you a 'flat top' haircut if you turn them up to the top setting and place your hair inside the safety guard.

- However tempting it may be, do not shake your fist at the sun. People who shake their fists at the sun tend to look insane, more importantly you might anger it then who knows what it might do.

MASSIVE POLICE CRACKDOWN ON MULTIPACK CANS SOLD SEPARATELY

Police forces across the UK are targeting shopkeepers who illegally separate fizzy drink cans from larger groupings.

OPERATION Orphan, budgeted at £16 million, raided more than 14,000 newsagents, convenience stores and mini-markets yesterday and made almost 20,000 arrests.

Chief Inspector Helen Archer said: "Every year, soft drink manufacturers lose hundreds of pounds in revenue because of shopkeepers splitting multipacks.

"What's hard for us to understand is that these villains run their empires with the collusion of the public.

"These cans are clearly marked, and anyone who buys them has a duty to report the vendor to the police.

"Tragically, it seems the British public would rather guzzle their Fanta without thinking of the human cost of their actions."

A newsagent and two members of the public lost their lives in a gun battle yesterday, with police reporting the trader had "nothing left to lose" having already been cautioned for selling a limited edition Peanut Lion after best before date.

Not to be sold separately under any circumstances, you filthy scum

Army to hold pistols sideways

THE British Army is to modernise its pistol-holding techniques with positions up to and including sideways.

The Army will train all soldiers to hold the standard-issue weapon horizontally in a bid to attract recruits who would otherwise join street gangs or the police.

A Ministry of Defence spokesman said: "Our current style of pistol holding is insufficiently masculine. Sideways will make our soldiers feel like giant, invincible erections."

But Wayne Hayes, a surly, ill-educated bastard from Doncaster said: "I'm not joining until they can teach me how to make a bullet swerve in mid-air."

Short men really are inferior, say tall scientists

Tall researchers have concluded that short men are inferior in every possible way.

THE report, titled *Look At The Teeny Tiny Men*, demonstrates that short men are less successful, have to sit on cushions to drive and are constantly simmering with resentment.

Project leader Dr Tom Booker, who is the ideal height of 6ft 3ins, said: "Remarkably, every one of our negative assumptions about short men turned out to be true.

"They are the Yorkshire Terriers of the human world: yappy, aggressive, annoying and easily shaken off a normal person's leg.

"We put a 5ft 5ins man in a room for 12 hours where food, water and entertainment were freely available, albeit on a shelf 7ft from the floor.

"Within hours he was screaming, leaping, tearing the furniture apart, and throwing his own faeces like a red-faced miniature hairless ape.

"In contrast, a normal man of 6ft locked in the same room for the same period happily got himself some crisps and a drink before settling down to watch *Pointless*."

The report recommends that short men be forced to wear muzzles in public, excluded from upscale venues by putting door handles higher up, and legally required to warn potential sexual partners of their substandard genetic material.

Booker warned: "However, it isn't a case of the taller the better.

"Every inch taller than 6ft 3ins a man is makes him 11% more freakish, and means he can only find employment in home removals, nightclub security or shelf-stacking."

Hermione should have married Jackie Chan, says Rowling

JK ROWLING has admitted that Hermione Granger would have been much happier married to martial arts legend Jackie Chan.

The Harry Potter author said the character's marriage to Ron Weasley was a mistake and would have led to mutual resentment, heavy drinking and repeated viewings of *Rush Hour 2*.

She added: "Hermione needed to be with someone on her level. She would have been dazzled by Jackie's lightning-fast hands and his ability to jump on to tables.

"And even though I forced her to marry Ron, I like to think that at some point she would have had an affair with Jackie Chan.

"Or possibly Shaft."

Pensioners incapable of pronouncing 'chorizo'

ELDERLY people cannot say chorizo without inserting a 't' sound, it has emerged.

New research claims the spicy sausage has become part of the UK's staple diet. However people over 60 still insist it is called 'choritzo'.

67-year-old Mary Fisher said: "I love a bit of choritzo. We have it on our pitzas when we go to Pitza Express."

Pronunciation expert Tom Booker said: "There's no point in telling them. Just go with it."

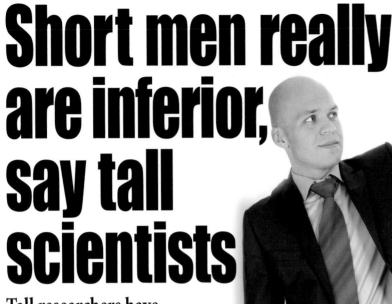

World wondering when it'll turn on Jennifer Lawrence

THE world's moviegoers are debating when they'll decide they can no longer stand actress Jennifer Lawrence.

Movie blogger Francesca Johnson said: "My projected date to start despising J-Law is June 24.

"I don't know what J-Law will do: perhaps appear in a film I don't like, or date someone I don't approve of. Or maybe even just gain or lose weight.

"Whatever it is, something will turn the high esteem I currently hold her in into a bottomless well of contempt and disgust that will be my core obsession."

Film critic Julian Cook said: "Fame can be a harsh mistress.

"But don't worry Jennifer. My love will be eternal, just like it used to be for Heather Graham when she was still young."

In Sweden she is considered homely

Sweden to become more stereotypical

Swedish ministers have announced a six-hour working day as part of plans to make their country more stereotypical.

THE policy is one of several designed to bring Sweden in line with the caricatured view of the country held by other nations, particularly Britain.

Prime Minister Fredrik Reinfeldt said: "Sweden leads the world in progressive social policy, but frequently visitors are disappointed that we don't spend all our time assembling Ikea furniture in the nude.

"From now on all Swedes will have to spend at least 20 hours a week doing Swedish things, such as having a sauna and beating themselves with twigs while feeling totally unashamed of their naked bodies.

"We will also be deporting any women who are not tall, blonde and stunningly attractive. This may sound harsh, but it's the only way to create the Volvo-driving, porn-using, smorgasbord-eating stereotype that the outside world loves so much."

Reinfeldt said other policies would include banning all music that was not Abba-style disco-pop, which would be a blow to the country's many rock musicians, hip hop artists and classical musicians, but would be popular with tourists.

Briton Roy Hobbs said: "I went on holiday to Sweden and for some unfathomable reason I didn't have sex with any Swedish women. Fortunately Thomas Cook apologised and gave me a full refund.

"I did see a man on skis taking a reindeer for a walk, but that was a pretty poor substitute for 14 nights of passion with blonde nymphomaniacs."

FEATURE

The Daily Mash Guide to ...
Keeping Warm this Winter

Winter is coming, in real life as well as in Game of Thrones.

Follow the tips below for the best chance of re-emerging blinking into the sunlight in six months' time:

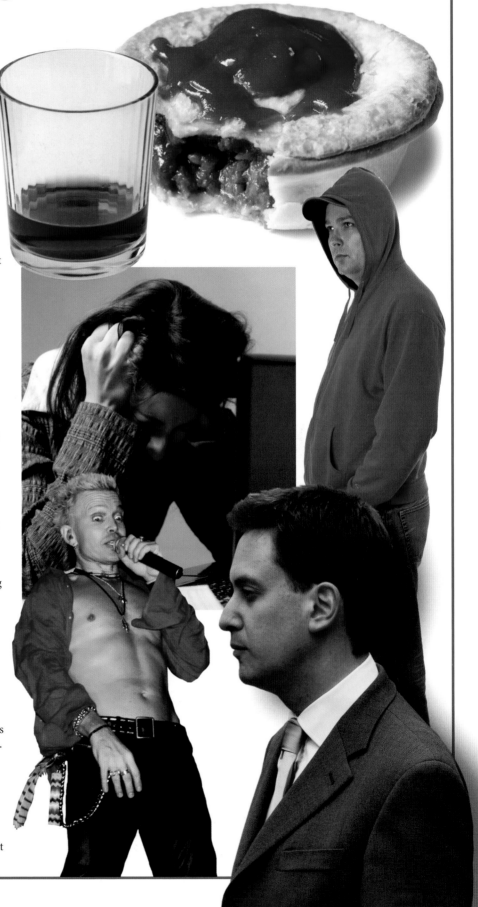

● **Get fat**
A good, thick layer of subcutaneous fat will make sure you're toasty all through the winter months and provide an energy reserve for when you can't afford food. Start gorging on cakes and pies now.

● **Get drunk**
Drinking spirits like whisky and gin can make you feel warm. In fact alcohol causes blood vessels to dilate, lowering core body temperature. But whatever, you still feel warm.

● **Work harder**
Too cold at home? Most employers will let you stay on at work as long as you continue being useful, for no extra charge.

● **Get Miliband to pay your bill**
If you're planning to vote Labour in 2015 then Ed Miliband's promised to pay your gas bill, so crank up the thermostat and get naked.

● **Look intimidating**
If you're worried about your annual heating bills, put on a jumper. If you put on a hoodie, you are either too young to worry about heating bills or too old to wear a hoodie.

● **Listen to warm music**
Listening to the right music will give a psychological feeling of warmth. Try *The Heat Is On* by Glenn Frey, *Hot In The City* by Billy Idol, *Disco Inferno* by The Trammps or *Blowtorch Slaughter* by Cannibal Corpse.

● **Smoke cigarettes**
Smoke indoors, because every winter several hundred people go outside for a fag and almost immediately freeze to death. Also a lit cigarette is a small fire, so encourage your children to gather around it and warm their tiny hands.

Teens being too soft for WW2 'not a massive problem'

The fact that young people would struggle to cope in World War Two may not be a problem, it has emerged.

DESPITE media commentators frequently arguing that modern teens lack the qualities required to win WW2, historians believe the chances of them having to fight in a 1940s global conflict are in fact quite small.

Historian Denys Finch Hatton said: "The main reason it doesn't matter is because of the linear nature of time.

"But if somehow World War Two was going to happen there'd be plenty of warning, like Angela Merkel spending all her time watching massive panzer parades instead of going to tedious EU trade meetings.

"We could probably still utilise our obese youngsters by building Spitfires with bigger cockpits and a charger for their phone so they could text each other during dogfights.

"Spending thousands of hours playing *Call of Duty* has given teenagers lightning reflexes, thorough knowledge of WW2 weapons and a virulent hatred of Germans and the Japanese.

"The horrendous levels of abuse during online play have also probably rendered them impervious to all but the most brutal interrogation by the enemy."

WW2 veteran Roy Hobbs said: "During D-Day I literally shat myself, but they never put that in the war films for some reason.

"Still, I did nick loads of things from abandoned houses, so it wasn't all bad."

It is technically over

D-Day veterans thank Britain for becoming so self-absorbed

THE veterans of D-Day have marked the 70th anniversary by thanking Britain for becoming shallow and worthless.

The soldiers who liberated Europe from fascism stressed we had done them proud with our relentless focus on money, celebrity, clothing and football.

Bill McKay, 92, said: "Just before I stepped off the landing craft, bullets flying past my head, I turned to my mate Trevor and said, 'I do hope future generations won't take this for granted in any way, because that would be a total pain in the arse'. And Trevor agreed with me wholeheartedly.

"As I recall, he speculated on what seemed an unlikely scenario whereby Britain becomes utterly self-absorbed and complains about absolutely everything. He may even have used the phrase 'little shits'. "

McKay added: "Of course we were both shouting at each other because of all the bombs going off, so I may have misheard him, but I'm pretty sure it was 'little shits'.

"Anyway, Trevor and I kept in touch and over the years we have laughed about how those unlikely predictions came true. I'm just kidding, we're incredibly angry about it."

But Tom Logan, a 33 year-old marketing consultant from Hatfield, said: "It's only because of those brave men that I can be so shallow, materialistic and complacent.

"I'd imagine being ruled by Nazis does tend to keep you focused on the things that really matter."

ENGLAND WINS WORLD CUP

England have basically won the World Cup.

Fans and pundits say a 2-0 friendly victory against Poland is essentially the same as winning the World Cup and beating all the other teams is now just a formality.

TV football pundit Bill McKay said: "Beating Poland shows England can succeed at the highest level of international football, so we've won the World Cup. That's just common sense.

"There isn't much point in holding the rest of the matches in Brazil because FIFA are probably planning to give us the trophy as soon as they've put our name on and given it a polish.

"To be honest, I had my doubts about whether England would ever win the World Cup again. Imagine how stupid I feel now."

England supporter Stephen Malley said: "Me and my mates got a load of cans and partied all night with the Lightning Seeds at full volume, until someone threw a petrol bomb through the window."

Today England manager Roy Hodgson arrived at FIFA headquarters in Zurich to collect the trophy, but was told that a legal technicality required England to take part in, and win, the actual tournament.

Hodgson said: "I'm hoping this can be resolved quickly, because we need the trophy for the victory parade on Saturday. Otherwise we'll have to make our own with a tennis ball glued to a Pringles tube."

England have mountain to climb in poor piece of scheduling

FOLLOWING defeat by Italy, the England football team now faces an ill-timed trek up Brazil's tallest mountain.

Critics claim the treacherous ascent of Pico da Neblina should wait until the team's World Cup obligations have been concluded.

Manager Roy Hodgson said: "I agree that the timing is not ideal but the lads fancied it so it was all booked in before we came. If we cancel now we lose our deposit for the guides and jeeps."

Pico da Neblina is known for the high risk of a parasitic disease called onchocerciasis, or river blindness, which Hodgson admits is a concern.

Gerrard walks alone into jungle

ENGLAND captain Steven Gerrard last night walked into the Amazon jungle on his own.

The midfielder, whose errors have cost Liverpool the title and England the World Cup, disappeared into the darkness of the rainforest without looking back.

Teammate Daniel Sturridge said: "Stevie's been talking a lot about the South American tradition of the Jaguar King, in which the previous leader is sacrificed at the end of his period of rule.

"He's also saying that perhaps he would concede fewer tackles if he was entwined in snakes."

Gerrard is expected to return before Tuesday's game against Costa Rica, completely naked and painted in the garish colours of the green-winged macaw.

It wasn't as if Suárez bit a child, say experts

Experts have stressed that Luis Suárez bit a large Italian footballer and not a tiny child.

WITH many calling for the Uruguayan striker to be jailed, doctors said Suárez's victim had already made a full recovery, despite pretending to be dead.

Sports injury specialist, Dr Julian Cook, said: "The key difference between biting an opponent and going in hard with your studs up is that biting them is much more interesting for everyone involved.

"The actual biting injury is usually pretty mild. Mr Suárez is a medium-sized Uruguayan, not a Sumatran tiger."

Dr Cook added: "If Mr Suárez had ran towards the crowd, grabbed a small child and bit it on the face, then yes, by all means phone the police.

"But, as far as I understand, Mr Suárez has no desire to bite infants. He just wants to bite large professional footballers. Preferably Italian.

"Despite what Alan Shearer may tell you, that's absolutely fine."

Meanwhile, many fans have welcomed the incident and called on Fifa to legalise biting on a trial basis.

Stephen Malley, from Peterborough, said: "There is something dark and primal about it which I find utterly irresistible.

"Give both teams 10 bites each. And it has to be below the waist."

The Italian footballer, shortly before he died

Military defeat by Britain key to World Cup success

BEING beaten by Britain in a military conflict is the secret to winning the World Cup, it has been claimed.

Finalists Germany and Argentina have both been defeated by Britain in wars, a blow which may have spurred them on to sporting success.

Military historian Tom Logan said: "In 1945, Germany waved the white flag. Nine years later, they've won the World Cup.

"In 1982, Britain ejected Argentina from the Falkland Islands. Four years later Argentina lift the trophy. With Germany as finalists wouldn't you know.

"Humiliation on the battlefield at the hands of Tommy Atkins seems to act as a great motivator to these nations.

"Italy, there's another one."

England squad begins 10-year voyage home

ROY Hodgson and his England team have boarded a ship to begin their epic journey back to the UK.

The squad, who will row a two-masted trireme, expect to be home within a month but have embarked on an odyssey that will last a decade.

Hodgson said: "First of all we'll ~~be blown off course to the Falk-~~ land Islands where Adam Lallana will be sodomised by a one-eyed man in a cave.

"That is mainly his own fault, though, because he disguised himself as a sheep.

"Next, a mysterious sorceress will transform the entire squad into pigs for a bit. I challenge you to spot the difference.

"The beautiful sirens who'll attempt to lure us to our deaths will be ignored, because the lads are used to that kind of thing and also because they've all got their headphones on.

"Finally, we'll arrive back in England to find that ten years have passed, that all their clubs and WAGs have long since replaced them and that their names ~~are pretty much forgotten.~~

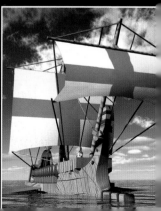

UNPARALLELED BRITAIN BATTLES HAVOC CRISIS

- Britain's chaos crisis is no longer paralleled.

- The strewn Atlantic has littered warnings as derailed trees battered standstill.

- In trains, commuters wobbled and lashed hurricanes caused flooded travel havoc.

- Meanwhile, more than 2,000 armies have pumped out Staines.

- Red alert weather science confirmed Britain is now entirely abandoned to a whole month of severe in less than hours.

- A prime minister said: "Unparallel the havoc! Battleground the levels!"

If only church was like this every Sunday

Floods to be followed by giant wolf eating the sun

Meteorologists have confirmed that Ragnarok, the Viking apocalypse, will happen on Sunday.

WEATHER experts confirmed the event after reading up on Norse mythology, which describes extensive flooding followed by monster-based chaos.

A Met Office spokesman said: "Just when you thought things were calming down a bit weather-wise, a giant wolf is going to swallow the sun.

"Meanwhile Thor is to battle a world-girding serpent and the gates of Hell will open, its denizens spilling forth to wreak havoc on earth.

"Don't travel unless absolutely necessary."

Eleanor Shaw, from Leeds, said: "The Vikings predicted the Earth falling into the sea which is pretty much what's happened to my nan's house in Warminster.

"I'll be staying in with a grab bag of Doritos and watching the action live on Ant & Dec's Ragnarok."

Slayer fan Wayne Hayes of Nottingham said: "To be honest I couldn't get into that whole Mayan apocalypse thing in 2012 – too ethnic for me – but this one's gonna rock.

"There's going to be dwarves fighting ice giants and a bone ship full of skeletons. Basically it's the full on metal apocalypse depicted on my favourite t-shirt."

News mainly pictures of waves

NEWS editors have confirmed that they are mostly going to be doing pictures of waves for the time being.

A BBC spokesman said: "There's just so many types of wave – frothy, foam-y, crescent-shaped and tidal to name but four."

Daily Mail editor Paul Dacre said: "Waves are eye-catching yet terrifying, rather like women in general.

"Also people tend to stand too close to them, and we will be encouraging readers to despise those individuals for their stupid recklessness.

"That's until one of them gets swept away. Then we will mourn their tragic loss – especially if that person wanted to be a model."

Environment Agency to fill Somerset with piranhas

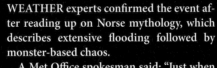

THE Environment Agency is to step up its attack on Somerset with more than two million carnivorous fish.

Piranhas will be released into the flooded Somerset Levels, turning thousands of acres of once productive farmland into an insatiable frenzy of blood.

A spokesman said: "Let this be a warning to all who would dare accuse the Environment Agency of incompetence."

The move is part of the environmental watchdog's multi-million pound bid to overtake the Arts Council as Britain's deadliest quango.

Your problems solved, with *Holly Harper*

Katie is a competent horsewoman with huge breasts

Dear Holly,

It may be coincidence; it may be fate, but I notice that Katie Price has become single again at the same time as me. As far as I can see she is a competent horsewoman, an expert business person and has massive jugs to boot. Who cares if she is awfully vulgar? Should I give her a call anyway?

Prince Harry
Kensington

Dear Harry,

Just be careful. Whilst people often say that opposites attract, sometimes we need to be mindful of extreme differences. That's the lesson my granny learned when she got a kitten to keep her dog Bilko company. Granny was hoping it would turn out like The Incredible Journey; unfortunately it ended up being more like Deliverance. Poor Tootles just wanted a quiet life, but that was never going to be possible with an overly affectionate Yorkshire Terrier in the vicinity. Thankfully, Tootles is completely healed now and living with a nice goldfish who respects his personal space.

Hope that helps!

Holly xx

The most powerful wedgie ever performed

Dear Holly,

The most important qualities for a leader are a belief in organic farming, a disdain for modern architecture and a talent for watercolour landscapes. Unfortunately I've been caught slagging off Vladimir Putin as a man with none of these attributes and even compared him unfavourably to Hitler, who at least did the watercolours. Now he's coming to get me. I'm scared.

Prince Charles
London

Dear Charles,

There's nothing worse than knowing the biggest bully in school is gunning for you and has told everyone that when he finds you he will cut you clean in half with the most powerful wedgie ever performed on a human being. You are forced to change your hairstyle, wear dark glasses and avoid the playground at all costs. The worst part about it all is living in a constant state of high alert, never sure when the fateful blow will fall. Best thing to do is face the situation head on rather than spend the rest of the school year hiding in the PE cupboard at playtime. Stand tall, don't let the bully intimidate you and, most importantly of all: go commando.

Hope that helps!

Holly xx

Your astrological week ahead, with Psychic Bob

Aries
21 Mar-19 Apr
As a xenomorph, when you watch the film *Aliens* it's about trying to bring up a family while being hassled by soldiers.

Taurus
20 Apr – 20 May
If family values are the glue that holds society together, resentful drunken get-togethers are the Swarfega that dissolves it again.

Gemini
21 May-20 Jun
As of midday today Gemini will be discontinued as part of our ongoing cost efficiencies. You are now an Aquarius.

Cancer
21 Jun-22 Jul
After a week with no caffeine it's really made a difference – you constantly feel knackered and annoyed, like you just helped a total arsehole move house.

Leo
23 Jul-22 Aug
At the first use of the phrase 'plays to the rhythm of the samba', take the orange pill as directed. You will go to a better place.

Virgo
23 Aug-22 Sep
While the cat's away, the mice will play. Although given the amount of holidays cats can afford it's really not very long.

Libra
23 Sep-23 Oct
If your morning commuter train is anything to go by, there's a new breakfast cereal on the market made of faeces and sadness.

Scorpio
24 Oct-21 Nov
Time to face step nine in your 12-step programme – trying to remember where you parked your car.

Sagittarius
22 Nov-21 Dec
Your opium addiction is not 'taking some time out to smell the flowers'.

Capricorn
22 Dec-19 Jan
Legs is your favourite ZZ Top song about a woman learning how to walk again after a spinal injury.

Aquarius
20 Jan-19 Feb
For Lent, you've decided to give up resisting the urge to strip naked and scream at passing traffic at a busy intersection smeared in toothpaste.

Pisces
20 Feb-20 Mar
Your local vicar seems unimpressed when you wake him up at 6am on Monday to show that your scrotum sort of looks like Jesus.

Science mostly made up

Most scientific discoveries are fabricated in order to get money and fame, a scientist has revealed.

PHYSICIST Professor Julian Cook said he and fellow scientists invent all their findings in order to get grants and BBC2 series.

Professor Cook said: "Take that story about DNA evidence showing that early Homo sapiens went around having rampant sex with other species.

"There's no way you could find that out just using a bunch of bones. Even Poirot couldn't do that.

"So you just look at the bones and go 'mm – shagging'. Suddenly you're all over the newspapers and on telly, the money's rolling in and you've got a wardrobe assistant asking you which blazer and jeans combo you want to wear on Jonathan Ross.

"Real science is incredibly boring, so it's better to claim that a gi-ant meteorite is heading for earth, or that killer robots are going to take over.

"There's no way you're going to meet Fiona Bruce if you're just looking at microbes through one of those little desk telescopes."

Science historian Mary Fisher said: "Sir Isaac Newton made up gravity because he wanted to be famous but wasn't any good at singing or acting.

"The world is actually full of tiny sucking creatures that keep everything stuck to the floor, but you don't want to know that because it's rank."

She added: "Most human 'knowledge' is just a form of theatre. For example Brian Cox only has one GCSE in woodwork, his main credentials are memorable hair and a pleasant manner."

Newton used his 'Third Law of Motion' to impress girls

Gay computer is old people's worst fear

A COMPUTER that talks in an effeminate male voice is the biggest fear of the over-70s.

The Institute for Studies found that old people who previously spent their ample spare time worrying about homosexuals and technology were now anxious about an amalgam of the two.

83-year-old Tom Booker said: "I've heard about these Apple Gaypads that talk in a Frankie Howerd sort of voice and say rubbish like 'Ooh you just turned me on' and 'Plug it into my rear socket, go on'.

"They'll have them in schools and turn all the little kiddies queer."

Pensioner Susan Traherne said: "If gays moved in next door they'd probably have raucous parties with men rubbing oil on each other, but at least I could nail the bedroom windows shut.

"However the laptop my son got me could use gay internet sites to invite them all into my home, unlocking the doors with its computer powers so they can come in and bugger it."

British Gas smart meter switches all your stuff on when you're not there

NEW British Gas 'smart meters' wait until you go out and then switch on all your appliances.

The meters have been programmed to waste as much electricity as possible at the most expensive time of the day.

Consumer expert, Martin Bishop, said: "If you were to sneak back into your house you would find the telly and the stereo on full blast, the kettle boiling, the oven on and an empty washing machine on a repeating spin cycle.

"But you wouldn't be able to sneak back because the smart me-

ter knows exactly where you are and switches everything off just before you come home."

Jane Thompson, who has a smart meter installed in her Stevenage home, said: "It does feel that the house is now possessed by an ancient spirit that wants to steal from me."

FEATURE

Simon Cowell's top tips ...
for Mothers

People talk about the pressure new mums are under.
But the fact is: if you can't handle it, you shouldn't be here.

1. Breast vs Bottle Feeding

Okay, there's no right or wrong way to feed your baby.
But I'm not gonna sit here and tell you you're doing
it right, when clearly you're doing it wrong. Only very
few people really get this. Look, I breastfed all my
children, from Harry 'Biter' Styles to Matt 'Blocked
Duct' Cardle. I know the stress of the dreaded 8am
start and the agony of angry, engorged mammaries.
But there comes a time when I don't want to feel like
a couple of milk bags for some mewling pest. My
body is beautiful – and sexual. It's time I reclaimed it
for me.

2. Reconstructive Vaginoplasty

Okay, I'm gonna give you some advice here. Childbirth is
stressful so it's only natural to suffer some loss of tone. But
deal with it. When I go to executive lunches at Fox network,
I need to know I can sneeze with supreme confidence and at
maximum volume. But you don't need a surgeon to give you
that edge: you just have to get that pelvic
floor back up out of your gusset and
tight around your ribcage where
it belongs. A good exercise is
to abruptly stop urinating
mid-stream. Remember
to ensure a colleague is
nearby because if no one
sees you doing it, they
just assume you can't. If
you're at the staff urinal
and suspect they aren't
paying enough attention,
stop mid-flow, stare at
them until you're satisfied
they are, and then release
the remainder of your
stream.

3. Phonics

Phonics is a sham – a complete
waste of everyone's time. At the
end of the day the only things that
matter are the way you sound and
what you look like. This is why I'd be
doing my offspring an unkindness
if I said he didn't make noises like a
seagull going through a Dyson. To
me, it seems he's just opening his
mouth and blasting the first thing
that comes into his head. Where's
the originality? He is quite literally
murdering the English language.
But… I have to say in a weird way,
I quite like him. He reminds me of
Adele.

988 types of craft ale
page 90

Soft play & the mighty Spartan
page 99

Chris Martin's dream
page 105

the dailymash

www.thedailymash.co.uk

RANDOM ACTS OF FOUL-MOUTHED CRUELTY

Monday 2015

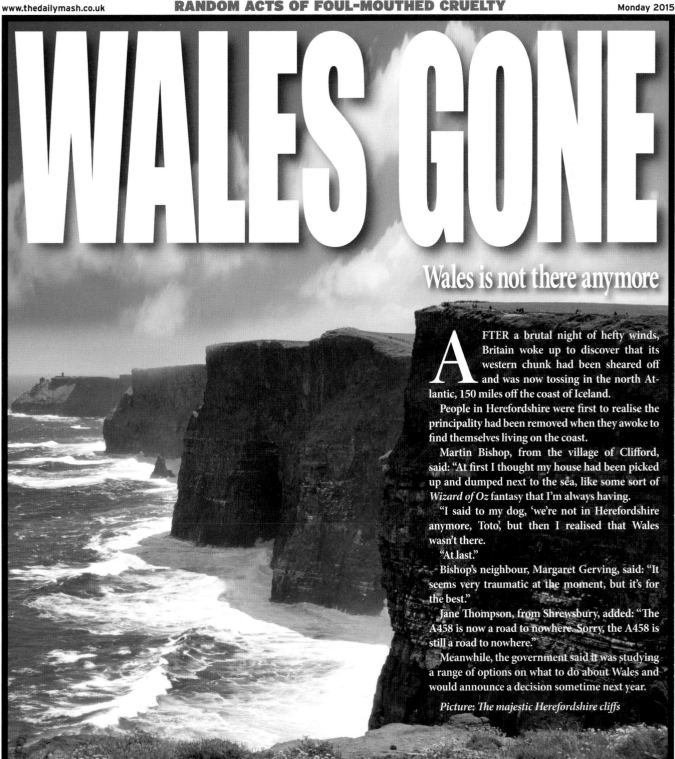

WALES GONE

Wales is not there anymore

AFTER a brutal night of hefty winds, Britain woke up to discover that its western chunk had been sheared off and was now tossing in the north Atlantic, 150 miles off the coast of Iceland.

People in Herefordshire were first to realise the principality had been removed when they awoke to find themselves living on the coast.

Martin Bishop, from the village of Clifford, said: "At first I thought my house had been picked up and dumped next to the sea, like some sort of *Wizard of Oz* fantasy that I'm always having.

"I said to my dog, 'we're not in Herefordshire anymore, Toto', but then I realised that Wales wasn't there.

"At last."

Bishop's neighbour, Margaret Gerving, said: "It seems very traumatic at the moment, but it's for the best."

Jane Thompson, from Shrewsbury, added: "The A458 is now a road to nowhere. Sorry, the A458 is still a road to nowhere."

Meanwhile, the government said it was studying a range of options on what to do about Wales and would announce a decision sometime next year.

Picture: The majestic Herefordshire cliffs

Everyone too up themselves to make the tea

She'll drink it but she's not fucking making it

Workers are going without hot drinks because everyone in the office thinks they're above making tea, it has emerged.

THE traditional drinks round has become a 'tea deadlock' as colleagues would rather die of thirst than lower themselves to heating water and pouring it into vessels.

Sales assistant Tom Logan said: "I badly want some tea. But I see myself as management material so I won't do what is basically manual work.

"Sure I could just make a single cup of tea for myself but that's a bit 'potential serial killer'."

He added: "And I can't bring a Thermos because owning a Thermos is a tacit admission that you are into dogging."

Logan's colleague Emma Bradford said: "I would participate in tea making but only as a group effort within a team-building context.

"Alternately I would project manage a round of hot drinks, or oversee tea preparation in a freelance consultant capacity."

The tea deadlock is particularly endemic across boring industries like financial services, where there are lots of insecure spivs. But even work experience people are no longer comfortable boiling a kettle.

19-year-old 'intern' Nikki Hollis said: "Making tea is against my human rights. I might burn myself, and also I should be running the company because I have a blog about sunglasses."

Professor Henry Brubaker said: "It may seem like a trivial thing, but this demonstrates perfectly why humanity will soon destroy itself."

Racist nans now in charge

PARTY leaders are to meet with prejudiced nans after it emerged they were responsible for the UKIP landslide.

The nans, who loathe foreigners and live to be 400, now constitute about 89 per cent of the electorate.

David Cameron is to meet with influential 86-year-old Mary Fisher later today, although she has already warned him that he is not coming in if his shoes are mucky.

The pair will discuss issues including 'other races', why they keep changing the names of chocolate bars, and next door's tree which is now so tall it nearly touches the telephone wires.

Fisher said: "I've made a list of all the races that want sending home, which is basically all of them apart from the Asian man who drives the Dial-A-Ride bus.

"He can stay. Not his family though."

Today declared Take An E at Work Day

MILLIONS of Britons are taking pills at work to commemorate the life of 'godfather of ecstasy' Alexander Shulgin.

Chemist Shulgin, who died this week, was instrumental in developing the drug that made repetitive dance music and stupid hats accessible to heterosexual white people.

Home secretary Theresa May said: "Ecstasy changed British culture forever, making football hooligans hug and launching highly profitable dance clubs that pretended to have a no-drugs policy.

"So it is only fitting that we should all get on one today. I double dropped fluffy old school White Callies shortly before making this speech.

"I feel nice, not sexual but loving with a warm body buzz."

It's all very special and amazing

Everyone else's life better than yours

Your life really is not as good as that of any other human, experts have confirmed.

RESEARCHERS into quality of life found that the depiction of other people's existences on social media and in celebrity news media was entirely representative of their amazingness.

Professor Henry Brubaker of the Institute for Studies said: "You might think these things are contrived for maximum impressiveness, but everyone else is genuinely having a great time, all of the time.

"Beside having fulfilling and well-paid jobs, loving families and fascinatingly varied sex lives,

the things they get up to are just such a laugh.

"For example, last weekend while shopping at a charming flea market in Amsterdam, marketing executive Tom Logan and his attractive girlfriend found these old security guard hats.

"They wore them all day as they cycled around the city's historic attractions on vintage bikes, like a pair of sexy comedy characters.

"Then they had a massive dinner."

Professor Brubaker also highlighted 28-year-old Emma Bradford, whose Twitter profile

describes her as 'mother, teacher, cupcake evangelist'.

He said: "That's two proper things followed by an amusingly light-hearted thing. She doesn't take herself too seriously because the various brilliant aspects of her personality are perfectly balanced.

"In conclusion, life is like an amazing non-stop party that's going on in the room next door. You can hear the muffled sounds of laughter, but the door is always locked."

Badgers take Swindon

Britain is top place to live, claims sarcastic think tank

GOVERNMENT forces have fallen back from positions in Swindon and Wiltshire, abandoning the town to the Badger Army.

The Department of Agriculture has cancelled planned new fronts in the Badger War to concentrate forces on defending the vital M4 corridor.

Defence analyst Julian Cook said: "The bad-

gers have followed the sinkhole offensive with a series of incursions into Swindon, taking the town street by street. The government might want to ask itself if it really believes it can win a ground war in Wiltshire."

Badger general Nathan Muir said: "For Swindon, badger law is now the only law. Reading is next."

THE Paris-based quality of life experts said: "We particularly like the food in your country, because frying imparts such a deliciously oily texture.

"Also your town centres are great, they feel so safe and welcoming on a Friday and Saturday night, especially at those lovely corporate nightclubs, or after a successful game of your national sport, soccer.

"Obviously the work-life balance, friendly muscular dogs and the weather are great too."

CRAFT ALE PUB HAS 988 VERY SIMILAR TYPES OF BEER

An East London 'craft ale' pub offers almost a thousand largely indistinguishable artisan beers.

THE on-trend hostelry, which has its own micro-brewery and is run by young men with tattoos, boasts of having the most bewildering selection of similar ales in the capital.

Landlord Tom Booker said: "Thanks to our commitment to traditional brewing techniques, we've been able to develop a massive range of ales going from light brown to slightly darker brown.

"They all taste of beer but in a very slightly different way.

"Boring corporate pubs only offer four or five types of pint. That's not enough choice to make the ordering process really long-winded."

Customer Emma Bradford said: "I like how you can try a small sample, before nodding knowledgeably as if you can tell 'Hoxton Sky' from 'Butcher's Hook'.

"Actually I just go for the one that has the most colourful label."

28-year-old Wayne Hayes said: "When I'm with friends I recommend 'Soldier's Arm' and 'Terrier', for no other reason than it makes me look like I know something about something.

"I do the same sort of thing with steaks, pretending I know what a Hereford cow looks like."

Public unsure what to do with info about big shops' sales figures

REPORTS of big shops' sales figures have left Britons baffled and mildly anxious.

Mother-of-two Emma Bradford said: "The news keeps telling me that Marks & Spencer has sold less clothes.

"Is that bad? Or is it good because it means there's more chance of getting pants in the size I need?

"Why am I being given this piece of information?"

Office worker Stephen Mal-

ley said: "I am supposed to feel I've let Marks & Spencer down by shopping in Primark?

"Is Waitrose good and other shops evil? Is that it? What's going on?"

RBS confirms it's still run by the most gigantic bastards imaginable

THE Royal Bank of Scotland just wanted you to know that it remains disturbingly immoral.

The taxpayer-owned bank was keen to give 200% bonuses to its professional gamblers amid worries you may have temporarily forgotten it was being run by demons.

A spokesman said:

"Although we obviously don't need the bonuses they are symbolic of our hot desire to lay waste to your pitiful, ordinary lives.

"Next year, regardless of our level of failure, we're going to ask for 300% via a note stapled to the forehead of an old woman in a wheelchair."

Football is confirmed as team sport

Winning at football requires eleven good players, experts have confirmed.

AFTER Germany lifted the World Cup by having a team of people behaving as a collective, coaches have been asked to focus on more than one person at a time.

Footballologist Wayne Hayes said: "Received wisdom suggested that Argentina would win 'because of Messi', but he didn't have the ball for 98 per cent of the time so that didn't really work.

"Predictions that he would play keepy-up for ten minutes before hitting a 40-yard thunderbolt into the top corner of the net using his penis now seem a little unrealistic."

Suspicions that victory requires more than just one player were raised when Brazil lost 7-1 by repeatedly passing the ball to Neymar despite him not being on the pitch.

Earlier in the tournament England showed the shortcomings of the individual-based strategy when the one player you are relying on is awful.

This World Cup has nothing on 1954, say football hipsters

FOOTBALL hipsters have dismissed suggestions that the current World Cup is the greatest of all time, insisting it is vastly inferior to Switzerland '54.

Martin Bishop, from Peckham, said: "Anyone who compares Holland versus Spain to the 'Miracle of Berne' is frankly delusional.

"1954 had everything: a goal-per-game average of 5.38, the Magical Magyars, and a cutting-edge, Bauhaus-meets-Mondrian logo."

But football blogger Joseph Turner insisted that the World Cup had gone mainstream by the 1950s, adding: "Italia '34 was Italia '90 without the branding.

"I'd bet my Dukla Prague away kit Martin Bishop has never even heard of Oldrich Nejedly."

Relief as easily-stereotyped nation wins World Cup

FOOTBALL fans and pundits have expressed relief that World Cup discussion can focus on joyless efficiency.

Tom Logan, a 29-year-old fanatic, said: "You know where you stand with the Germans. They're emotionless, keen on engineering and probably about to invade somewhere despite pretending to be cool now."

Football journalist Julian Cook said: "I'll probably write a piece comparing the German victory to an Audi gliding down an autobahn to a sausage festival.

"And I'll definitely crowbar Kraftwerk and sauerkraut into it."

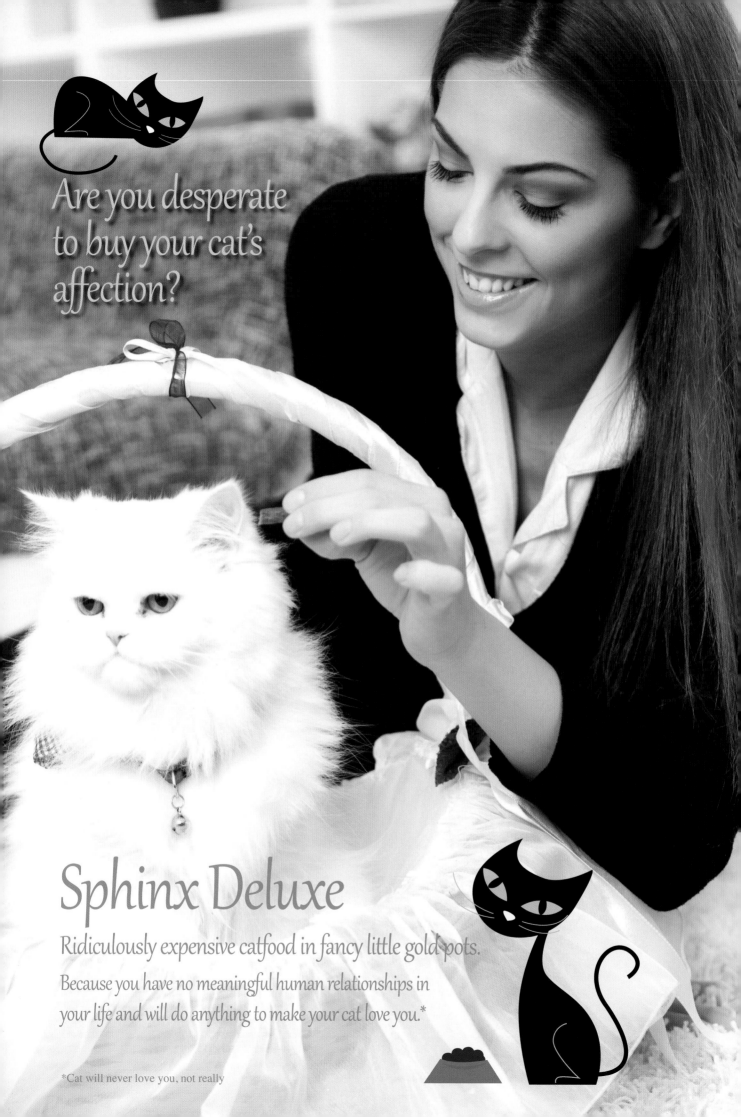

HEALTH
NOT THAT IMPORTANT

Your health is not especially important, according to a new study.

AFTER weeks of conflicting dietary advice in the media, researchers at the Institute for Studies concluded that health was over-emphasised compared to other lifestyle factors like pleasure.

Professor Henry Brubaker said: "Having a long life is all very well, but what if that life is utterly tedious?

"Happiness is impossible to quantify but resting heart rate and body weight are, which is why really dull people obsess about those things.

"They are still going to die though.

"If you compare someone who exercises every day to someone who gets pissed every other night, the former might live ten or 15 years longer.

"It's not a lot when you think about it. It's questionable whether it's worth bothering."

Professor Brubaker added that health was particularly unimportant as most humans will never amount to much anyway.

"For the vast majority of us, what we do work-wise is fairly routine and doesn't involve discovering or inventing anything particularly great.

"So if we die a bit early it's not that big a deal, humanity isn't particularly going to lose out."

Absolutely fine

No good chocolate bars since 1981

EVERY chocolate bar invented since the Wispa has been either uninspired or disgusting, it has emerged.

The Institute for Studies found that there had been no worthwhile additions to the chocolate bar canon since Wispas came out over three decades ago.

Professor Henry Brubaker said: "Wispa is the last 'top tier' chocolate bar, and even that's essentially a pretentious Aero.

"Some might argue for Boost, but Boosts are impossible to eat. Absurd levels of chewiness mean I've seen discarded Boosts with teeth embedded in them."

Brubaker highlighted the green Boost with guarana in it and limited edition mango Bounty as examples of a creatively-barren industry veering towards the grotesque.

"The clean, militaristic Yorkie is the pinnacle of chocolate design, although the Double Decker is perhaps the most radical, being based on a bus."

Alpha male 'just a thing some men think they are'

Win, achieve, annoy

Men who believe they are alpha males are deluded, it has emerged.

THE Institute for Studies studied self-styled alpha males and found them to be undistinguished men with larger-than-average watches.

Professor Henry Brubaker said: "One thing that's clear is that anyone who thinks they're an alpha male isn't one.

"94% of these people are involved with either the selling or marketing of mobile phones, an industry which is inherently unmanly.

"They live in new-build flats they can't really afford and read *GQ* magazine for tips on how to find favour with their boss.

"The true alpha male is a yeti-like beast – wild, unphotographed and possibly mythical.

"It's better to classify men as 'idiot' or 'not idiot.'"

Stephen Malley, 31, said: "I'm an alpha male because I shout at people, for example laundrette staff and anyone else who isn't allowed to answer back because of their employment terms.

"Also I have a weirdly clean serial killer-type home and a remote control that operates nine different gadgets and can make my favourite Olly Murs track play in any room including the airing cupboard.

"Additionally I have previous convictions for stuff involving rohypnol, but that's all in the past now."

Pulled pork 'does not make you more manly'

FASHIONABLE meat meals like pulled pork, steaks and 'barbecue' do not confer manly qualities, it has emerged.

It had been thought that the large, oozing meat dishes consumed in restaurants with exposed brickwork and quasi-American names were making men stronger, braver and more capable in battle.

Professor Julian Cook, from Roehampton University, said: "We took a group of men, fed them nothing but pulled pork and 28-day-hung rib-eye steaks for a month, then dropped them on the Orkneys with just pocket knives to see if they would survive.

"They all died."

Meat restaurant entrepreneur Tom Booker said: "Pulled pork is over anyway. These days it's all about yanked pork or tugged pork."

The meatiest meaty meat

I'd have eaten toddler myself if it was smaller, says 'hero cat'

Cat

America's 'hero cat' has admitted she would kill humans if they were small enough to fit in her mouth.

CAT Tara won the hearts of simpletons by apparently saving a four-year-old from a dog attack.

The tabby carnivore said: "I did it because, much as I hate kids, I hate dogs more.

"I've no idea what the kid's name is. A 'name', as you so whimsically call it, is just a noise to signal the availability of food."

Describing the perceived bond with her owners, the cat said: "I don't recognise the concepts of ownership, family or friendship. I simply go where the protein is.

"I never think about the bipeds that feed me, except in idle moments to imagine them rodent-sized with me slowly plucking their limbs off one by one as they wail in agony."

As a reward for her brave exploits, heroic Tara was honoured by being allowed to throw the first pitch at a baseball game: "I can't throw things because my arms don't swing, this is basic anatomy.

"You may as well ask a cow to drive a golf cart."

Tara added: "For the avoidance of any further confusion, I am a cat. Cat. Cat."

US and Europe on brink of passive-aggressive letter to Putin

THE United States and Europe have warned Vladimir Putin to watch his post box for a passive-aggressive bombshell.

A White House spokesman said: "We could say something like, 'oh, we didn't know you were going to invade Ukraine, maybe someone forgot to tell us'.

"Or there's, 'these days we tend to do things via the United Nations – it's in New York, so you probably didn't know about it'.

"And, of course, there's always, 'we're not trying to tell you what to do, we're just trying to help'."

A Kremlin spokesman said: "President Putin greatly enjoys receiving letters from effeminate Western men. He likes to read them out in a high-pitched voice.

"This sounds like it could be a really good one."

Mad Men to conclude with creation of Um Bongo ad

THE NEW series of *Mad Men* climaxes with the writing and recording of the Um Bongo advert.

The Um Bongo campaign, widely recognised as the pinnacle of advertising, is revealed to be rhythmically inspired by the bouncing breasts of Christina Hendricks.

A show insider said: "We speed through the 1970s, seeing Don Draper come up with the R. Whites ad when back on the booze and the Smash ad while idly playing with two ladles.

"But by the mid-80s, he's an old man struggling to recapture past glories who hasn't had a hit since the Tefal Men."

With the Um Bongo campaign his only hope, a desperate Draper drops six tabs of acid at the Bronx Zoo and hallucinates a 20-minute CGI sequence of the animals themselves making a tropical fruit drink.

Found slumped against the hippopotamus enclosure muttering 'it all starts with that guy...' Draper works on the ad through the night, browbeating Peggy to find something for the marmoset to pick and a 'decent goddamn rhyme for mango'.

In the last scene of the final episode, Draper is shot and killed on a business trip deep in the Congo by furious natives who have never tasted the drink.

LIVING EACH DAY LIKE IT'S YOUR LAST ACTUALLY A TERRIBLE IDEA

What the hell do you think you're doing?

Behaving as if you're going to die tomorrow will lead to humiliating and possibly deadly situations, experts have warned.

FOR decades tattoos, Hollywood films and people at backpackers' hostels have recommended living every day like it is your last.

However 31-year-old office worker Tom Logan said: "There's this girl in marketing I've always liked, but I was scared she was out of my league. Then I watched the film *Point Break* on cable and decided to 'live in the moment'.

"I approached her in front of the whole team and said 'there's something I need to tell you', then I grabbed her, leaned her backwards like in those pictures of returning American GIs and kissed her fully on the lips.

"Now I'm getting done for sexual harassment. I've lost my job and the local paper has labelled me a sex pest.

"I should add that this happened yesterday. Today is today, I am still very much alive, just having a total nightmare."

Stephen Malley, 28, said: "I punched my line manager and drove a sports car into a river, because of *carpe diem*.

"Now I am going to prison for two years, where I will continue to live on the edge but in a less fun way."

Philosopher Mary Fisher said: "People should live every day like they're going to be alive for the remainder of their natural life span.

"It's obvious really."

Fried food ban could kill Scottish children

SCOTTISH children may die if schools can only serve them deep fried food once a week, it has been claimed.

Proposals to limit school canteens to one battered meal every seven days have been condemned as lethal to Scottish pupils, who have a genetic need to consume oily, beige-coloured things.

Glasgow school cook Susan Traherne said: "Batter contains the nutrients that are essential to survive in the hostile Scottish climate.

"If this madness spreads north of the border, most kids will not last out the first week. They will start jittering and collapse, and you won't be able to revive them with your 'salads'."

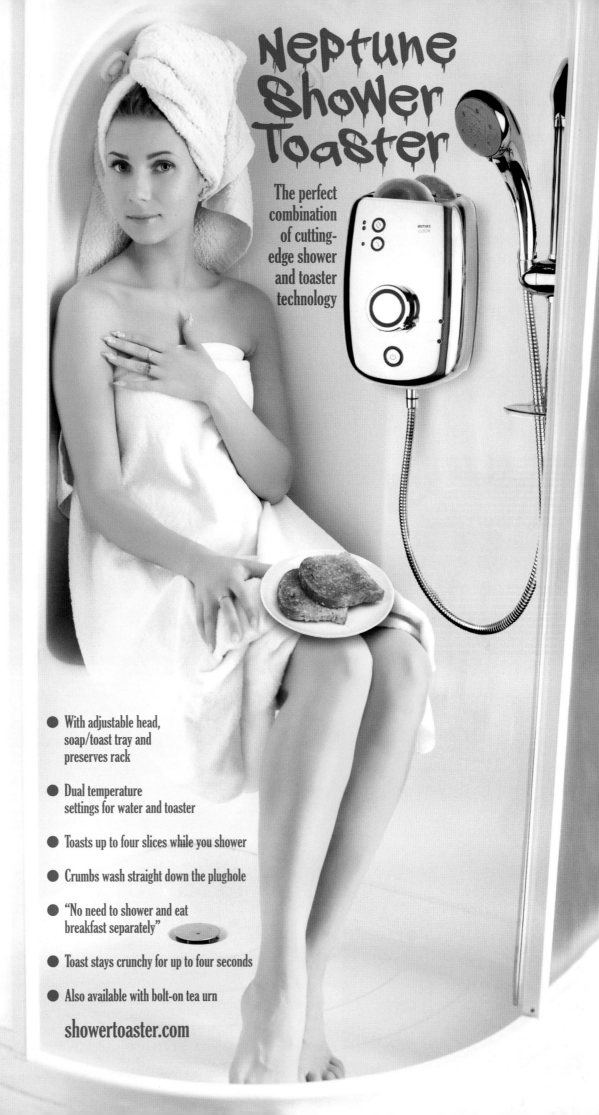

An open letter from Royal Mail

We're watching you from in here

Dear People,

Over the last few months, we've watched the popularity of open letters grow and grow.

From Sinead O'Connor to Roger Waters, it seems everyone wants supposedly one-on-one communications to be read by absolutely everybody then discussed at length in the newspapers.

Why, this very morning there's a wonderfully entertaining open letter in *The Times* from Eleanor Shaw of Harrogate to her husband detailing exactly when, where and why she's been having it off with the au pair.

But we're afraid there is a big problem with this new craze for open letters: we don't make any money from them.

If you're pissed off with someone, send them a letter personally and get a chain of correspondence going. Maybe get some other family members or legal representatives mailing them poisonous notes, or send them a creepy dead animal via our excellent Parcelforce service.

"Not my problem," you might be thinking. "After all, hasn't Royal Mail been privatised?"

Well yes, of course we have. But don't think for one second that our hand won't be straight in the taxpayer's pocket if our profits fall.

And you don't want to make us angry. You know where the phrase 'going postal' comes from? Do you want to see Postman Pat with a shotgun in one hand and a 'Sorry, you are fucking dead' card in the other?

It's time for you to re-acquaint yourselves with a little thing called an envelope. Write a letter, pop it in, put a stamp on while moaning about how much they cost these days and we'll get it to the recipient the next day, or month or whenever.

Remember, we get up earlier than you and we know where you live.

Yours, Royal Mail

King Leonidas's
trip to the soft play area

On this day I, King Leonidas, have come to Adventure Kidz soft play complex – where the heart of a true warrior is forged. This is Sparta.

Once inside, I remove my helmet for it is stifling and narrows my vision. I remove my shield for it is heavy, and throws me off-balance. I remove my shoes, for there is a big picture of a shoe with a cross through it. And then I run.

To my left is the ball pool. It is but an appetiser for a son of Sparta. I laugh in its face as I dive-bomb in, thrashing its coloured balls asunder. Some puny adversaries can flip one or two balls onto the carpeted area nearby, but a Spartan warrior can get them as far afield as the café, front desk, even car park.

Next, I infiltrate the toddler area – neormally barred from intruders by a formidable gate system. I wait for a feeble-minded patrolman to leave it unlocked, then advance. Once inside, I raze to the ground any structures

higher than two or three soft-bricks. Any structures of military value, such as forts, I save for occupation. It will be from their secure concealment that a ravenous king can indulge in activities normally taboo in the battle-zone, such as eating Quavers.

With a satisfied belly, I can deal with uprisings. To make an example, I march one particularly mouthy rebel up the perilous climb to the highest target of all: the 'giant death slide'. I dangle him by his ankles from its dizzying vertical drop and ask him again if he preferred things the way they were before. Ignoring his pleas, I cast him down to oblivion. There is no place for whining in Sparta.

True warriors are required to be engaged in conflict for many hours at a time and, with the

toilet facilities being literally over 800 miles away from the trampolines, I now appear to be sitting in a suspicious smelling puddle. But it was definitely not bold Leonidas who made this mess, no way. It was definitely Xerxes, because he is a stupid face baby man who is still in pull-ups.

As I leave the war zone victorious, I decide I must be rewarded. Who will buy me this chocolate doughnut? No-one is stepping forward which confuses me because as Leader of Free Sparta, I deserve it more than anyone else in the world. I start screaming with every fibre of my being. A destroyer of Persia has lungs like exploding volcanoes because within seconds I am the proud owner of not just a doughnut but a Yazoo as well. Tonight I feast with the gods!

Stocky dog disagrees with owner's claim that it doesn't bite

"I am pretty sure I do bite"

An aggressive-looking dog has dismissed its owner's claims that it would never bite anyone.

STOCKY, big-headed dog Bronco is often described by owner Tom Logan as 'soft as anything' and 'like a big puppy'.

However Bronco said: "Pretty much every time I meet a person, I find myself thinking about locking my huge jaws around their leg.

"Would I do it? I don't know. I guess I'm what you'd call unpredictable.

"In fact I had a moderately serious dust-up with a Boxer in the park last month.

"Tom seems to have conveniently airbrushed that from his memory.

"He is a rather irresponsible owner."

Tom Logan said: "He can look a bit scary, particularly when he's growling and going completely mental with slobber flying everywhere, but he's just a pussycat really."

Bronco said: "Tom needs to start telling people to stay the fuck away from me.

"Especially people wearing hats. I really am not into people wearing hats.

"They make their heads look a weird shape which scares me and makes me uncontrollable."

Columnist running out of feminist perspectives

GUARDIAN columnist and blogger Nikki Hollis is running out of things on which to have a feminist perspective.

Hollis is increasingly having to shoehorn feminism into subjects like rail travel, dog ownership and crisps.

The 31-year-old writer said: "I realised things were getting desperate when I wrote a piece criticising fishing for being a male-dominated hobby.

"But maybe women just don't like fishing because it's fucking boring. Also, who cares?

"Men need to pull their fingers out and find some new ways of oppressing women so that I can write about it."

Hollis' recent articles have included criticism of outdated gender roles in *Downton Abbey* and a piece that bemoaned the lack of female flashers.

People born in 1980s to spend their retirement fleeing from euthanasia robots

PEOPLE now in their 30s will spend their retirement fleeing from government robots programmed to kill old people.

Professor Henry Brubaker of the Institute for Studies said: "An ageing population means that Britons can no longer expect to spend their retirement playing golf, going to Florida and obsessing about the parking space outside their house.

"By the 2030s the government will have an army of 'reaperbots' programmed to hunt and kill the billions of older people who have outlived their economic usefulness.

"The robots will be able to smell your DNA and have hypodermics for fingers. Also they will be strong enough to punch holes in walls in their pursuit of you.

"On the plus side, in the future there will be massive tellies and strawberry flavoured crisps."

MIKE TINDALL TAKES VITAL STEP TOWARDS SEIZING THE THRONE

Former England rugby captain Mike Tindall has strengthened his bid to seize the throne from Queen Elizabeth.

THE birth of his child by the Queen's granddaughter Zara means Tindall has the beginnings of his own royal bloodline and can now persuade the army to back his claim.

Royal analyst Julian Cook said: "Tindall has been frustrated by Britain's weak leadership and has been desperate to depose the Queen and purge the royal court.

"Now that he has successfully merged his genes with the House of Mountbatten Windsor, senior generals will take him more seriously."

As a former England rugby captain Tindall already has the ancient right to hunt boar in the Royal Forest and maintain a garrison of 50 archers.

But now insiders say he will quickly amass a vast army, forcing the royal princes Charles, Andrew and Edward to flee to Calais.

Cook added: "Choose your allegiance Britain. It is a time of swords."

Wales beaten at rugby by country that doesn't even like it

WALES is in turmoil after being beaten at rugby by a country that is indifferent to the sport.

The rugby-obsessed nation suffered a crushing 29-18 defeat at Twickenham by an England team that only does it for a bit of fun.

Welshman Gwyn Morgan said: "Rugby is our main 'thing' and the very backbone of our national identity, so to be beaten by a country where it is only watched by retired doctors is utterly devastating.

"This sport is pretty much all we have apart from singing in choirs, and even that's been hijacked by the BBC and that twat Gareth thingy."

England rugby coach Stuart Lancaster said: "It felt good seeing the boys win. Up to now it's only been a hobby, but I could really get into this niche football variant."

England still doing cricket

DESPITE overwhelming evidence that it just isn't for them, England is still persisting with cricket.

After being repeatedly demolished by Australia, England suffered fresh defeats against the West Indies at a different kind of cricket, suggesting that any variation on the game is beyond them.

However England announced plans to continue 'cricketing' for the rest of the year because it is fun.

Giles Clarke, England's cricket-in-chief, said: "Cricket's great, you get to wear your pyjamas all day and there's free sandwiches.

"I suppose it'd be nice to win a game or two, but that's not really what cricket's about, is it?"

You should have heard some of the other poster ideas, says Farage

UKIP leader Nigel Farage has rejected criticism of the party's latest poster campaign, assuring people they have absolutely no idea.

MR FARAGE revealed the party's grassroots members had offered their own suggestions, adding: "Sweet. Jesus."

He said: "One of them suggested me in a paramilitary uniform standing on top of a mountain, with the slogan, 'Men of England, Touch My Destiny'.

"There was also the man snatching a baby from a pram, with the instruction that he look 'very obviously semitic'.

"Then there was 'the pile of skulls'.

"The person who sent that one in writes everything in capital letters and suggested we 'POSITION IT OUT-SIDE PRIMARY SCHOOLS'.

"Meanwhile, another member suggested a simple photo of a fully-erect black penis, but with no slogan, insisting the image 'encapsulates absolutely everything we are trying to say'. "

Mr Farage also revealed the party's next set of posters will include a swarthy looking man in a dirty vest, a man with a Union Jack painted on his face, blowing his brains out, and an array of suspicious-looking tropical fruits with the slogan 'Mangoes? Papayas? Whatever Next?'

"But covered in blood"

Lloyds horse quits

THE Lloyds horse has stepped down after losing confidence in the bank.

Stallion Roy Hobbs was an iconic figure in the financial services industry, but became increasingly disillusioned in the wake of the PPI scandal.

He said: "As a horse, I shared none of the corporate values of Lloyds but was happy to persist with my role in exchange for a paddock, treats and a fence to rest my chin on.

"I began to get pissed off when they started their own in-branch radio station. No-one wants to hear All Saints' *Never Ever* when they're writing out a paying in slip. But mainly it was that they're a bunch of bastards."

A Lloyds spokesman said: "It's a blow, but already we were thinking of switching the horse for a lizard."

UKIP councillors told they can't withdraw Doncaster from EU

NEWLY elected UKIP councillors have discovered they are not allowed to remove their borough from the European Union.

The local councillors, whose skills include patriotic fervour, will now be forced to spend the next five years calling for Union Jacks to be painted on wheelie bins.

Norman Steele, the new leader of UKIP-controlled Doncaster Council, said: "I was proud to announce earlier today that Doncaster will be freed from the yoke of EU membership with immediate effect.

"I have now been informed this will not be possible. Same goes for my plan to build a 200ft wall around the city to keep out the Bulgars."

Former BNP councillor Stephen Malley said: "When I was elected in 2009 I couldn't get anyone deported and there was no money for my spectacular torchlight rally.

"However, I was able to deny the Holocaust during a meeting about mobility scooters."

It's not raining

SNP FURY AS MET OFFICE CLAIMS SCOTTISH WEATHER NOT VERY NICE

Scottish nationalists have reacted with fury after a Met Office study found the country's weather was really quite unpleasant.

ACCORDING to the research Scotland gets 'a lot' of rain, often accompanied by wind, and the amount of sunshine is 'statistically insignificant'.

But SNP leader and first minister, Alex Salmond, dismissed the study as a 'pathetic attempt by unionist weathermen to talk Scotland down'.

He added: "The Met Office thinks Scotland is too wee and too wet to be a successful nation. An independent

Scotland would enjoy the same climate as other small northern European countries, such as Norway and Iceland."

Salmond insisted that, based on 'perfectly reasonable assumptions' Scotland's weather would improve by four per cent in the 10 years after independence, delivering an annual per capita increase of six-and-a-half hours of sunshine.

The SNP leader also highlighted figures which showed that Dunbar, a small town on the east coast, was already one of the sunniest places in Britain. Bill McKay, from Dunbar, added: "It's raining. Again."

A Met Office spokesman stressed it was 'pretty sure' its figures were correct, adding: "We use these little beakers to measure rainfall."

Cameron gets injections for trip to Scotland

DAVID Cameron has demanded 'all the jabs going' ahead of his trip to Scotland.

A Downing Street spokesman said: "It is part of the prime minister's duties that he visits countries in the developing world. Unfortunately many of the locals are quite infectious.

"He wanted the injections for smallpox, diptheria, scarlet fever and 'anything you can get from human bites'."

Salmond accuses JK Rowling of sorcery

SCOTTISH National Party leader Alex Salmond has accused JK Rowling of casting demonic mind-spells.

As the Harry Potter author gave £1m to the pro-UK campaign, Salmond said she was a 'voodoo woman'.

Rowling hit back, saying that Salmond was minimising the risks of Scottish independence, while stress-

ing that was a 'fairly straightforward statement' rather than a 'wizardy incantation'.

But Salmond replied: "It is the spell of 'reasonablacorum'. And did you notice that when she said it, she sounded a bit like a snake?"

Pro-independence campaigners backed Salmond, claiming that in

her past evil lives Rowling was a slave who collaborated with the Confederacy and a Nazi spy who reported directly to Joseph Goebbels.

Martin Bishop, from Fife, said: "And now she slithers among us, with her darting tongue and massive, unpatriotic houses.

"I still like the films though."

Chris Martin's meat dream
And I think we both know this is the end.

Your eyes, previously so full of life and laughter, are now dull, defeated and sunken
– the way I always imagined they might have looked inside Kevin Spacey's box at the end of Se7en.

And you ask me, after all that we've been through, do I still believe in magic?
Oh, yes I do! Because what else could explain your remarkable meat hat?

How, if magic did not exist, could two minutes ago your hair and head have been that of a normal woman's,
but now from nowhere a generous fistful of steak tartare has appeared there,
topped with a raw egg whose yolk is all yellow, yes, like the stars.

I ask you how you've done this. Was it from LK Bennett or perhaps River Island?
But you now seem more upset than ever, your mouth opens wide and you cry like your heart is slashed.
But inside your mouth is an entire black pudding supper, every tear rolling down your cheek,
an 8lb joint of gammon. What witchcraft is this?

I'm in a daze, I don't know what's real and what's not.
The room spins, I hear ringing in my ears and everything seems so far away.
I stagger to the door, lost, broken, severely anaemic.

I get on my Segway and ride 'til my knuckles bleed and I start to get seasick,
all the way to my best friend Madonna's house.
She offers me a table upon which I can perform ashtanga yoga to soothe my aching soul.
I take the snooker, she takes the foosball. I ask her what a man's to do.
No doubt her words to me are wise, but though her lips move, I cannot hear her voice.
She is doing the crab, exposing each of her fascinating chakras.
But her seven centres of spiritual power have been replaced with huge beefburgers.
Mesmerised, I look closer and see that someone, probably a health professional, has drawn big purple
arrows pointing to them, each one is surrounded with exclamation marks like halos of pure chagrin.

And if you were to ask me, after all that we've been through.
Do I still believe in magic? Oh yes, yes I do.

Because I've been to B&Q. And I bought this barbecue.

Pope attacks Queen with bottle

POPE Francis tried to bottle the Queen yesterday after a comment about Henry VIII sparked a fight.

Previous royal visits to the Vatican have been conducted on an 'agree-to-differ' basis, but the monarch was goaded when the Pope made an offhand comment about her vast wealth.

The Pope greeted the Queen by asking if she had enough money yet and the Queen replied that Henry VIII could have got a 'quickie divorce' by bribing Pope Clement VII with a carriage full of altar boys.

After a brief silence the Pope broke the bottle of Balmoral whisky he had been given and lunged at her.

A Buckingham Palace spokesman said: "One minute they were exchanging gifts and the next they were wrestling on the ground with Prince Philip holding back the cardinals telling them 'they had to work this shit out'.

"Neither had time to take their rings off, so when they'd finished their faces looked like five pounds of raw mince."

CofE calls for Christian meat packaging to show Jesus eating a sausage

Eat a sausage in a church

The row over faith-based meat has escalated with Anglicans demanding that packaging shows an image of Jesus eating a large sausage.

The Archbishop of Canterbury insisted secular meat is 'no longer feasible' and that supermarket shoppers should be able identify Muslim meat, Christian meat, Hindu meat and Voodoo meat.

He said: "Jesus wanted everyone to enjoy meat, particularly sausages. It was the main reason he was crucified.

"I fully respect Islamic meat faith, Hindu beef dogma and the Jewish Sin of Bacon, as well as Buddhist meat-free reincarnation magic and the Voodoo chicken thing.

"But Christians deserve the same respect for their meat religion."

He added: "As for how the animals are killed, I'm not a vet, but have we tried hitting them over the head with a large, metal cross?

"Like I say, I'm not a vet."

Meanwhile, supermarkets have offered a compromise which would involve meat packing showing a photo of the abattoir employee who killed the animal.

Tom Logan, a marketing consultant, said: "We could have a picture of 'Brian' giving a big 'thumbs-up', accompanied by a few words telling us something about him – he's married to 'Helen', he enjoys cycling and his favourite film is *You've Got Mail*.

"Consumers could follow their favourites on social media and have conventions every year where they gather at a three-star hotel and watch 'Geoff' kill a pony."

Kate wins over Australia with anti-Kiwi racism

"Imagine being married to one of them"

THE Duchess of Cambridge has been taken to Australian hearts after a series of increasingly racist comments about New Zealand.

Kate has made headlines across the continent by charmingly insulting Kiwis as lazy, backwards farmers who punch themselves in the face when trying to tell the time.

Australian journalist Eleanor Shaw said: "From the moment she touched down, and remarked how wonderful it was to be in a country where sheep at least get bought a drink before sex, Oz has fallen in love with Kate.

"Her Kiwi impression – a pinched face and a whining voice demanding a slice of lolly cake – has turned ten thousand republicans into royalists.

"And when she told the Prime Minister that the haka is just how New Zealanders take a dump because their toilet seats are too filthy to touch, we were delighted.

"She's really winning hearts and minds."

Struggling badger cull may switch to cats

The government cull may switch to cats as badgers are quite hard to kill.

THE controversial badger cull has proved difficult to execute because badgers live underground, actively avoid humans and can run very quickly for an animal with such short legs.

David Cameron said: "Cats are just as problematic as badgers but in a different way.

"Cat turds make kids go blind. Also you can be stroking a cat and it will suddenly bite your hand, for no reason.

"Plus cats are everywhere, and can be summoned by shaking a box that contains cat biscuits.

"If we could thin out cat numbers that would definitely be an achievement."

Marksman Tom Booker admitted: "Badgers are very elusive.

"You can follow the badger prints for a bit and then they just disappear. They're like ghosts or something.

"Perhaps they are the spirits of our ancestors. I don't know, to be honest they're starting to creep me out."

Mother-of-two Emma Bradford said: "I dislike this idea, because most cats have names.

"My mum always told me 'never kill anything with a name' and I've stuck to that."

They have a spiteful demeanour

Johansson film is thought-provoking, haunting and has breasts in it

UNDER the Skin is an elegiac masterpiece where you see Scarlett Johansson in the nuddy, according to critics.

The Guardian critic Peter Bradshaw said: "This story of a voluptuous alien predator is like a social-realist take on Cronenberg's best work.

"Also there are boobs in it. Not just boobs in fact, you get to see the lot, it's awesome."

Telegraph reviewer Robbie Collin said: "It's a masterpiece, combining echoes of Polanski with situationist techniques and a nod to the cosmic horror of HP Lovecraft.

"And there's hooters in it a couple of times, once around the 27 minute mark, then again later.

"It's like the thinking man's Species meets the iconic Jamie Lee Curtis bathroom scene in Trading Places. That good."

Sheepdogs condemn glass ceiling in the workplace

NO sheepdog has ever made the transition to shepherd, it has emerged.

Collie Tom Logan said: "I'm out there busting my arse every day, running like fuck in zig zags until all the sheep are in their pen.

"I only have to look at a flock of sheep and they all sit down. No one knows ovine psychology like I do.

"Why then am I sleeping in an outbuilding next to a sack of potatoes? Because I'm not a biped.

"I could easily run my own flock. I've got great ideas for a range of organic marmalade too, but nobody ever listens.

"Every time I try to throw a few ideas in the mix, somebody shuts me up with a biscuit."

Public warned not to acknowledge festival wristbands

People wearing expired festival wristbands are a limitless source of tiresome drug anecdotes, it has been claimed.

THE general public has been warned against mentioning the wristbands to their wearers, who are constantly ready with monologues that are ostensibly about music and drugs but really just about how amazing they are.

A police spokesman said: "'Banders' will pretend to have forgotten to remove their festival passes because they are free spirits who live in the moment and are too spontaneous to own a pair of scissors.

"Clearly this is bullshit. They're itching to tell you about some beautiful experience in the healing field that changed them in ways you, a hapless slave of the system, can barely begin to comprehend.

"They deserve to be hit with a stick."

28-year-old bander Tom Logan said: "Oh, this Glastonbury 2014 VIP Access All Areas wristband in limited edition cerise? I forgot I even had it on.

"But since you ask I had the most beautiful Glasto experience where I took some acid, thought it hadn't worked then woke up in my yurt at 6am tripping my tits off.

"I walked up a hill where there was a robot sculpture made of old cars and sat watching the clouds. But they weren't normal clouds, they were deep clouds.

"Then a girl wearing fairy wings gave me some of her Orangina and we went to see some bands."

The police spokesman said: "Also be wary of people wearing a 'festival crew' t-shirt in the pub or anyone driving a van that has a 'Crew Parking Shambala 2009' sticker on the windscreen.

"It's probable they will be fake hippies, but genuine dickheads."

A portal to tedium

Queen destroys aircraft carrier

THE Queen has destroyed Britain's newest aircraft carrier after hitting it with a bottle of whisky.

The monarch had planned to christen the Queen Elizabeth at the Rosyth dockyard in Scotland, but moments after the bottle made contact, the £3 billion vessel shook violently and collapsed into a heap of twisted metal.

The Queen stood silently before the wreckage and then shook her head slowly and mumbled 'what the fuck is wrong with this country?'.

Meanwhile, prime minister David Cameron shrugged, thanked the Admiral of the Fleet for the cup of coffee and went straight back to London.

A Ministry of Defence spokesman said: "The ship builders forgot to use rivets. These things happen. It's only money."

Girls on shoulders refusing to get down

HUNDREDS of women are still being carried around on mens' shoulders as they leave Glastonbury.

Young attractive females who perched on shoulders during the festival have decided that they want to be held aloft on a permanent basis.

Nikki Hollis, 23, has been on the shoulders of her obedient male friend Tom Logan since Dolly Parton played on Sunday.

She said: "I only got up here in the hope of being filmed by lecherous BBC cameramen but it's ace.

"Everyone literally looks up to you and I can even sleep if I lean forward. I kick him once to walk and twice to stop.

"I'm going into work like this tomorrow."

However girl-carrier Tom Logan said: "It hurts so much, I can't hold out much longer. My back is soaked in sweat and urine.

"I want to put her down but I fancy her to a tragic extent, even though this sort of obedient behaviour is exactly why she'll never go out with me."